IN THE LINE OF FIRE

SOCIAL INSTITUTIONS AND SOCIAL CHANGE
An Aldine de Gruyter Series of Texts and Monographs

EDITED BY

James D. Wright

Larry Barnett, **Legal Construct, Social Concept: A Macrosociological Perspective on Law**

Vern L. Bengtson and W. Andrew Achenbaum, **The Changing Contract Across Generations**

Thomas G. Blomberg and Stanley Cohen (eds.), **Punishment and Social Control: Essays in Honor of Sheldon Messinger**

Remi Clignet, **Death, Deeds, and Descendants: Inheritance in Modern America**

Mary Ellen Colten and Susan Gore (eds.), **Adolescent Stress: Causes and Consequences**

Rand D. Conger and Glen H. Elder, Jr., **Families in a Changing Society: Hard Times in Rural America**

Joel A. Devine and James D. Wright, **The Greatest of Evils: Urban Poverty and the American Underclass**

G. William Domhoff, **The Power Elite and the State: How Policy is Made in America**

Paula S. England, **Comparable Worth: Theories and Evidence**

Paula S. England, **Theory on Gender/Feminism on Theory**

Richard F. Hamilton and James D. Wright, **The State of the Masses**

Gary Kleck, **Point Blank: Guns and Violence in America**

David Knoke, **Organizing for Collective Action: The Political Economies of Associations**

Dean Knudsen and JoAnn L. Miller (eds.), **Abused and Battered: Social and Legal Responses to Family Violence**

James R. Kluegel, David S. Mason, and Bernd Wegener (eds.), **Social Justice and Political Change: Public Opinion in Capitalist and Post-Communist States**

Theodore R. Marmor, **The Politics of Medicare** (*Second Edition*)

Clark McPhail, **The Myth of the Madding Crowd**

Clark McPhail, **Acting Together: The Organization of Crowds**

Steven L. Nock, **The Costs of Privacy: Surveillance and Reputation in America**

Talcott Parsons on National Socialism (*Edited and with an introduction by Uta Gerhardt*)

Carolyn C. and Robert Perrucci, Dena B. and Harry R. Targ, **Plant Closings: International Context and Social Costs**

Robert Perrucci and Harry R. Potter (eds.), **Networks of Power: Organizational Actors at the National, Corporate, and Community Levels**

James T. Richardson, Joel Best, and David G. Bromley (eds.), **The Satanism Scare**

Alice S. Rossi and Peter H. Rossi, **Of Human Bonding: Parent-Child Relations Across the Life Course**

Joseph F. Sheley and James D. Wright, **In the Line of Fire: Youths, Guns, and Violence in Urban America**

David G. Smith, **Paying for Medicare: The Politics of Reform**

Martin King Whyte, **Dating, Mating, and Marriage**

James D. Wright, **Address Unknown: The Homeless in America**

James D. Wright and Peter H. Rossi, **Armed and Considered Dangerous: A Survey of Felons and Their Firearms**

James D. Wright, Peter H. Rossi, and Kathleen Daly, **Under the Gun: Weapons, Crime, and Violence in America**

Mary Zey, **Banking on Fraud: Drexel, Junk Bonds, and Buyouts**

IN THE LINE OF FIRE

Youths, Guns, and Violence in Urban America

JOSEPH F. SHELEY and JAMES D. WRIGHT

ALDINE DE GRUYTER

New York

ABOUT THE AUTHORS

Joseph F. Sheley is Professor of Sociology, Tulane University. Dr. Sheley is the author of *Understanding Crime, America's "Crime Problem,"* and *Criminology: A Contemporary Handbook.* He has published numerous journal articles. At present, he is continuing his investigation of patterns of firearm acquisition and use by juveniles.

James D. Wright is Charles and Leo Favrot Professor of Human Relations, Department of Sociology, Tulane University. He is the author of numerous journal articles and author (or coauthor) of over twelve books including: *Address Unknown: The Homeless in America; Under the Gun: Weapons, Crime, and Violence in America; Armed and Considered Dangerous: A Survey of Felons and Their Firearms; The State of the Masses* and *The Greatest of Evils: Urban Poverty and the American Underclass* (all: Aldine de Gruyter).

ALDINE DE GRUYTER
A division of Walter de Gruyter, Inc.
200 Saw Mill River Road
Hawthorne, New York 10532

This publication is printed on acid free paper

Library of Congress Cataloging-in-Publication Data
In the line of fire : youths, guns, and violence in urban America /
    Joseph F. Sheley and James D. Wright.
          p.   cm. — (Social institutions and social change)
    Includes bibliographical references (p. 000–000) and index.
    ISBN 0–202–30548–1 (cloth : alk. paper). — ISBN 0–202–30549-X
(paper : alk. paper)
        1. Juvenile delinquency—United States. 2. Urban youth—Crimes
against—United States. 3. Firearms—Social aspects—United States.
4. Gun control—United States. 5. Crime—United States.
6. Violence—United States. I. Sheley, Joseph. II. Wright, James D.
III. Series.
HV9104.I48   1995
364.3'6'0973—dc20   95–19598
                                                                                                  CIP

Manufactured in the United States of America

10 9 8 7 6 5 4 3 2 1

For Bernadette and Chris

CONTENTS

PREFACE

It is difficult to place any kind of positive spin on the issue of adolescents and guns in the contemporary urban context. Like everyone else, we would prefer that fewer kids owned firearms and that those who do were just hunters and sport shooters. In fact, neither perception captures the experience of the young males who participated in the research described here. Some were students in inner-city high schools; others resided in maximum-security correctional facilities for youth. Few seemed interested in hunting and sport shooting.

We have surveyed these youths about their guns because the media increasingly picture violence as a way of life for urban adolescents and locate the problem squarely within a rapidly expanding weapons arsenal for youth. We do not doubt the accuracy of this picture, but we also realize that it is grounded mainly in anecdotes that seem to be informing antiviolence policy—always a dangerous precedent. Our goal is to bring empirical evidence to bear on the issue of urban kids and guns. Is the phenomenon as widespread as the media suggest? If so, what kinds of firearms are juveniles obtaining? How do kids get guns and at what price? Why do youths carry and use guns: for crime, for respect, for protection? Is the problem an offshoot of drug use and trafficking? Is it confined mainly to gangs?

In The Line of Fire tries systematically to answer these questions. We have focused on adolescents who inhabit social environments that seem to foster gun violence: the contemporary inner city and the social world of the seriously criminal adolescent. We traveled to four states and to five cities within them to survey these youth. We began with confined juvenile lawbreakers and then moved our survey to inner-city high schools in large urban centers near the reformatories we had visited.

Given the volatility of the topic at hand, it is important that we balance our presentation of findings in this book with the observation that *most* inner-city adolescents do not own and carry guns. This holds even for those who attend classes in the particularly troubled schools in which we concentrated our study. Most simply are trying to get on with their lives as kids are everywhere. However, our findings indicate that their social world is not like that of kids everywhere. Very high percentages of their peers are carrying guns, and this convinces many more that they too need the protection—or sense of it—that comes with possession of a firearm. To the extent that their peers are engaged in criminal and drug-related activity, guns become yet more prevalent.

The level of firearm activity among our respondents has caused us to scrutinize carefully the oft-considered remedy for the problem: control of gun distribution at the retail level. The solution seems not to fit the problem. There is little that juveniles can now do within the law to obtain and carry guns. The large number of adolescents with guns in this society are getting them outside the law, from friends and family members and through a substantial and inexpensive underground supply. They do not *need* the retail market. Our look at kids and guns suggests to us a problem of such dimensions that it is time to shift attention from supply to demand. If demand remains high, it will be served even at higher costs for weapons. It is time to look at the larger structural and cultural forces that promote an environment in which substantial percentages of adolescents perceive a gun as essential to their survival.

The research reported in this book was funded by grants from the National Institute of Justice and the Office of Juvenile Justice and Delinquency Prevention. While we are grateful for their support, the conclusions we draw are ours alone and do not necessarily reflect the positions of our benefactors. A special note of thanks must go to Dr. Lois Mock of NIJ, who was especially helpful in the design and production of this study. This study would not have been possible without the assistance of the administrators of the schools and institutions we visited, and we are indebted to them. Dwayne Smith, our coinvestigator, deserves special thanks. Tulane University's Department of Sociology was immensely supportive. Finally, we acknowledge and appreciate the efforts of Hennessey Hayes, Zina McGee, Bryan Langs, Jerome McIntosh, Louis Corsino, Joshua Zhang, Derek Wright, Frank Bomaire, Stephen Feiler, and Al Sullen in the data collection and analysis phases of this project.

GUNS AND VIOLENCE AS AN
URBAN PROBLEM

Is this going to take long? I got someplace to go tonight.

—An eight-year-old Chicago boy, being questioned
by police after shooting a classmate in the spine
with a semiautomatic pistol, quoted in *Newsweek*

Violence committed by and against juveniles has come more and more to define the public's image of the crime problem and the larger political debate over anticrime policy. No longer adequately depicted as mere "juvenile delinquents," today's young offenders are frequently described as violent, hard-core felons. State legislators and local officials increasingly are making juveniles the target of their efforts to curb crime. Not so many years ago, police officers and school principals worried about young "hoods" who drank beer and carried brass knuckles and switchblade knives. Today, they are preoccupied with hardened youth dealing crack and carrying semiautomatic firearms (McKinney 1988:2; National School Boards Association 1993). It is a sobering possibility that many teenagers in today's cities know more about the technology and operation of a semiautomatic handgun than they know about personal computers or even automobiles. More disturbing still is the likelihood that their knowledge of firearms will prove more useful, at least as they see it.

Most people can appreciate, if only dimly, that cities—more precisely, certain parts of most cities (Rose and McClain 1990)—have become increasingly dangerous places, but few perhaps comprehend just how commonplace violence has become or how thoroughly it has penetrated the day-to-day routine of urban existence. A recent study of inner-city children ages seven to nineteen in Birmingham, Alabama, for example, found that 43 percent had personally witnessed a homicide or the body left in its wake (*Newsweek* 9 March 1992:29). Schubiner, Scott, and Tzelepis (1993) report that 42 percent of Detroit inner-city African-American youths, ages fourteen through twenty-three, had witnessed a

1

shooting or stabbing; 22 percent had seen someone killed (see also Fitzpatrick 1993). Similarly, 42 percent of a sample of Baltimore inner-city twelve–twenty-four-year-olds had witnessed a shooting; 25 percent had seen a stabbing; 23 percent had seen someone murdered (Gladstein, Rusonis, and Heald 1992). Finally, a survey of mothers in a New Orleans housing project found 71 percent reporting that their children had seen a weapon used, 49 percent that their children had seen someone wounded, and 39 percent that their children had seen dead bodies (Osofsky, Wewers, Hann, and Fick 1993).[1]

Giving these findings a somewhat more human face, consider the following sampling of newspaper stories concerning weapon-related violence involving youth in the nation's twenty-fifth largest city, New Orleans, during a recent eight-day period:

Wednesday: Jasmine Burton, a seven-year-old girl, is on her way to the store to buy bubble gum when gunfire breaks out. Jasmine is wounded in each of her legs. The injury to the right leg is superficial but the wound to the left leg is not. A six-hour operation saves her leg and she is in stable condition the next day, but she will likely walk with a limp for the rest of her life. Two other youthful bystanders (ages sixteen and twenty-two) are also wounded and sent to the hospital. Witnesses' accounts of the incident vary, but apparently there were five or six men shooting at one another. Police have no idea what the shooting was about.

Thursday: Ike is an eighteen-year-old high school senior, the star quarterback on his football team, and the recipient of a full-ride athletic scholarship to a major university. His "up from the projects" success story has a hitch, however. Ike has just been arrested on a number of charges, including armed robbery, and the police have confiscated a handgun and a sawed-off shotgun at the point of arrest; bail has been set at $188,500.

Friday: Undrell Hubert is a seventeen-year-old female high school student in the hospital with a stab wound to the abdomen. She and three other girls (ages seventeen, sixteen, and sixteen) had become embroiled in an argument at school. Police have no idea what the argument was about. As the argument became heated, one of the other girls pulled a knife from her purse and stabbed Undrell. The remaining two girls kicked Undrell after she had been stabbed and had fallen to the ground. Officials at the school were unavailable for comment.

Saturday: Djuan Hills, a two-year-old toddler, has died after being shot in the head with a .22-caliber revolver by his nineteen-year-old baby-sitter. The circumstances surrounding the incident are "mysterious." The sitter claims that the shooting was accidental, but his account appears "inconsistent." He has been booked on a charge of murder in the second degree. Djuan's father heard about the shooting while watching the television news in his jail cell, where he is serving time for possession of cocaine and illegal carrying of a weapon.

Sunday: "Public Housing Tour Jolts Leaders." A small group of civic leaders, protected by armed guards, walks through the city's Desire, Fischer, and St. Thomas housing projects accompanied by the city's top public housing officials. A "sock-clad girl of about six" says to her city's leaders: "They shot somebody right here [pointing to the ground at her feet]. They shot someone down there and down there too. A lady got shot down there and a man got shot down there [pointing her hands in both directions]. It's pitiful." It is customary at Fischer to decorate the buildings with the names of people who have perished in gun battles there.

Monday: One nineteen-year-old male is shot to death and another nineteen-year-old male is seriously wounded in a shoot-out with three other youths in the St. Thomas housing project, and an arrest warrant is issued for an eighteen-year-old male who is charged with the attempted murder of his girlfriend.

Tuesday: A twenty-one-year-old male is killed and three other men (ages nineteen, thirty-one, and thirty-five) are wounded in a brazen daytime drive-by shooting near a hospital. Based on the casings and bullets found at the scene, "it appears that semiautomatic weapons were used." Police have no motive for the shooting, no suspects, and in fact are unsure even who the intended victim was.

Elsewhere in New Orleans, a fourteen-year-old middle school student is accosted by two other youths who put a gun to the back of his head and steal his lunch money, two dollars. A nineteen-year-old male is riding his motorbike when several men open fire on him for no apparent reason. He is shot once in the buttocks and once in the back. Yet another young man (no age given) is held up by two youths armed with a sawed-off shotgun; the victim's jacket and tennis shoes are taken. Finally, a fifteen-year-old is accidentally shot in the left leg at a local public high school when the victim's fifteen-year-old cousin "handed the teen a bag containing a gun."

Wednesday: Jomo-kenyatta Joseph, a fifteen-year-old high school student, is shot in the head and killed. Herman Tureaud, also aged fifteen, is booked with first-degree murder; another male, age nineteen, is booked as an accessory to murder. The shooting is apparently the result of a fight involving about ten students and takes place in a school breezeway. School officials note that they use hand-held metal detectors on the campus to keep guns out of school and that they also have a full-time security guard, but apparently to no avail. The school where the shooting took place, incidentally, "is among the safer schools in the Orleans school district."

Elsewhere, a twenty-one-year-old male is shot to death with a .45-caliber semiautomatic near the site of an earlier drive-by shooting, an "apparent escalation of a blood feud." For the second time in six weeks, an early morning "gun battle" is reported to have taken place in a local elementary school near the Magnolia project. Atwon Harris (eighteen), Michael Anderson (nineteen), and Leonard Jones (twenty-one) are arrested by an off-duty police officer for stealing sports team jackets and tennis shoes from a group of young people at gunpoint. All three men are armed at the time of their arrest.

Youth Violence in Streets and Schools

The impression one gains from newspaper accounts like those just summarized is amply confirmed in recent statistics; indeed, quantitative evidence documenting the problem of youth violence is abundant. Homicide statistics for the past few years reflect record-breaking tolls in many U.S. cities (though the national trend over the past decade has remained relatively stable). Most of the increases in urban areas appear to have resulted from an upsurge of youth killing (mainly) other youth (Allen-Hagen and Sickmund 1993; Pooley 1991; *Scholastic Update* 1991; Witkin 1991). The number of persons eighteen and under arrested annually for murder increased by nearly a quarter from 1983 to 1988 (Miller 1989) and then increased again by nearly 50 percent between 1988 and 1990 (National Center for Juvenile Justice 1992; Snyder 1992).

Firearms appear implicated in much of the increase of youth homicides. The United States has approximately one hundred times more firearm-related homicides of young males than its nearest rival (France) among developed countries (Fingerhut and Kleinman 1990). Forty-eight percent of the deaths of black male teenagers in this country are firearm-related (for white youth, the comparable figure is 18 percent) (Fingerhut, Kleinman, Godfrey, and Rosenberg 1991). In 1990, 82 percent of the homicides of persons aged fifteen to nineteen were accomplished with guns; 76 percent of homicide victims between twenty and twenty-four died of gunshot wounds (Fingerhut 1993). By way of recent trends, for persons fifteen to nineteen years old, firearm-related homicides have increased more than 50 percent since the mid-1980s. Black males within that age group saw their rates approximately triple between 1985 and 1990—from 37 to 105 per 100,000; for black males twenty to twenty-four years of age, the rate changed from 63 to 140 per 100,000 (Christoffel 1992; Fingerhut 1993; U.S. Public Health Service 1992).

The concern with juvenile violence on the streets is matched by a related alarm over violence, especially gun-related violence, in schools (Leslie 1988; *Time* 1989). Interest in violence in schools certainly is not new (Bayh 1975; National Institute of Education 1978), though most systematic research suggested that the level of *serious* crime in schools in the 1970s and early 1980s was exaggerated (Duke and Perry 1979; Gottfredson and Gottfredson 1985; U.S. Department of Education 1984). The concern has returned more recently (Parker, Smith, Smith, and Toby 1991). While educators' journals and periodicals debated the *level* of school violence in the late sixties and early seventies (Thistle 1974), the same publications today offer articles urging school administrators to implement plans for dealing with the *aftermath* of violent incidents, for example, by providing emergency psychiatric counseling for students after an in-school slaying (Collison, Bowden, Patterson, et al. 1987). Print media articles about confiscations of firearms and attempts to prevent gun-related violence among high school students have become commonplace (Harrington-Lueker 1989; *New Orleans Times-Picayune* 1991; *U.S. News and World Report* 1990, 1993).

Recent analyses of the 1989 National Crime Victimization Survey supplementary data (Bastion and Taylor 1991; see also Whitaker and Bastion 1991) further support the picture of violence in the nation's schools. Of approximately twenty-two million students aged twelve to nineteen nationwide, 2 percent had been victims of violent crime (generally of a lesser type) in or around their schools during the past six months; this translates into more than four hundred thousand violent criminal episodes in and around schools in a single six-month period (U.S. Department of Justice 1991). About one in five students feared an attack at school; one in twenty avoided specific places in the school for fear of violence (see also Pearson and Toby 1991). Rates of violence were higher in schools where drugs were perceived as readily available and where youth gangs were present and active. Among those at highest risk of violence were males, blacks, and inner-city residents (Whitaker and Bastion 1991; see also Gottfredson and Gottfredson 1985).

Many now argue that schools no longer have distinct roles in the etiology of youth violence; rather they have become the physical locations where larger community problems are manifested (Sheley, McGee, and Wright 1992). Such factors as community size, crime rate, economic stability, and the racial composition of neighborhoods appear related to school crime. Gottfredson and Gottfredson (1985) found higher levels of victimization among those students reporting crime problems such as robbery, burglary, and gang wars in their neighborhoods. Hellman and Beaton (1986), in an examination of school crime, school characteristics, and community characteristics, found greater support for the effects of school characteristics (i.e., dropout rate, academic performance, school size) on crime among *middle school* students and more support for the influence of community characteristics (i.e., family structure, housing quality, crime rate in the neighborhood) on crime among *high school* students. Finally, research findings suggest that the presence of high-crime schools within high-crime communities intensifies the level of fear and apprehension experienced by many students (McDermott 1983).

Weapons in the Hands of Kids

Recent National Samples

A number of studies conducted since 1980 and using national-level data (or data pertaining to large areas of the United States) provide empirically grounded information about the prevalence of weapons use and violence among high school (or high school age) youth. A Bureau of Justice Statistics report (Rand 1990) based on analysis of 1979–1987 National Crime Survey data indicates that youth sixteen to nineteen years of age are at exceptionally high risk of victimization through a handgun crime. This holds for males and females, whites and blacks, and central city, suburban, and rural residents.[2] Analysis of 1985–1989 National Crime Survey data finds that a weapon (gun, knife, other, or "not ascertained") was used in 25 percent of the violent crimes committed against youth twelve to fifteen years of age and in 36 percent of the violent crimes against youth sixteen to nineteen years old (Whitaker and Bastian 1991). Guns were used in 20 percent of the weapon-related crimes against the younger youth and in 33 percent of those against the older youth. For the two age categories combined, 12 percent of the violent crimes committed in school, 21 percent committed on school property, and 37 percent of those committed on the street involved weapons.

Turning from victimization to the carrying of weapons, 3 percent of the males in a 1987 survey of 11,000 eighth- and tenth-grade students in twenty states reported bringing a handgun to school during the year preceding the survey; 23 percent reported carrying a knife to school (National School Safety Center 1989). Similarly, analysis of 1989 supplementary National Crime Survey data (Bastion and Taylor 1991) finds that 3 percent of the males and 1 percent of the females in a nationally representative sample of 10,000 students between the ages of twelve and nineteen had carried a weapon ("a gun, knife, brass knuckles, or things that could be used as weapons—razor blades, spiked jewelry") or other object ("capable of hurting an assailant") to school for protection at least once during a specified six-month period. In 1990, 20 percent of a nationally representative sample of 11,631 students in grades nine through twelve reported carrying a weapon at least once within the thirty days prior to being surveyed (U.S. Department of Health and Human Services 1991). Knives and razors (55 percent of the weapons reported) were more common than clubs (24 percent) or firearms (20 percent). Four percent of the students (21 percent of the black males) in the sample had carried guns during the previous month. Finally, a 1993 survey of 2,508 students in grades six through twelve in 96 schools nationwide found that 15 percent of the respondents had carried a handgun in the preceding thirty days; one in ten claimed to have shot a gun at someone (according to LH Research, Inc., in unpublished 1993 survey results obtained in a study conducted for the Harvard School of Public Health). [Notably, serious methodological questions have been raised about this study. Kleck (1993) argues that the data reflect a response-set bias whereby the respondents "were encouraged [via the introduction to the survey and the order of items] to provide responses indicating a gun violence problem more widespread than it really was."]

Selected Samples

Several studies utilizing selected samples during the past decade also provide insights into the issue of youth and weapons. In 1985, Fagan (1990) surveyed high school students and school dropouts in one select neighborhood in each of three cities (Chicago, Los Angeles, and San Diego) concerning a number of delinquent acts. He found that 18 percent of non-gang-affiliated males and 42 percent of gang-affiliated males had carried weapons (unspecified) illegally in the course of the previous year; percentages for females were fourteen and twenty-eight, respectively. His findings are not dissimilar to those reported by Fagan, Piper, and Moore (1986) and based upon samples of 660 male high school students and school dropouts from four inner-city, high-crime neighborhoods (one neighborhood each in Boston, Newark, Memphis, and Detroit). Of the high school students, 27 percent had threatened an adult with a weapon during the past twelve months, 20 percent had carried a weapon in a fight, 7 percent had used a weapon "to get something," and 9 percent had shot someone. Percentages for the school dropouts were 14, 28, 14, and 9, respectively. Similarly, Altschuler and Brounstein (1991) report that, of 387 ninth- and tenth-grade minority inner-city males they surveyed in Washington, D.C., in 1988, 27 percent had carried a concealed weapon in the past year, 11 percent had used a weapon to threaten another person, and 5 percent had "shot, stabbed, or killed someone."

Turning attention away from the metropolis, Asmussen (1992) reports that of 859 tenth-, eleventh-, and twelfth-grade students surveyed in a

Midwestern "small, urban, public school system," 6 percent had carried a weapon to school at least six times during the school year while 12 percent had done so between one and five times. Ten percent of the respondents had carried a weapon to school "during the past 30 days." Males were more than three times as likely as females to carry weapons. Knives were the most commonly carried weapon followed by handguns, clubs, and other weapons.

Regarding firearms more specifically, a 1987 survey of 390 high school students in Baltimore found that almost half of the males had carried a gun to school at least once (Hackett, Sandza, Gibney, and Gareiss 1988). Sadowski, Cairns, and Earp (1989) report that 5 percent of 664 teenagers they surveyed in 1987 in two suburban and rural southeastern school districts reported owning a handgun. A survey of fourteen- and fifteen-year-old male public school students in Rochester, New York, in 1990 found 6 percent owning a gun for "protection" (as opposed to ownership for sporting purposes; in the authors' opinion, protective guns primarily were handguns and sawed-off long guns). Seventy percent of the protective gun owners and 11 percent of the sport owners carried a gun on a regular basis (Lizotte, Tesoriero, Thornberry, and Krohn 1994).

Callahan and Rivara (1992), through a survey of eleventh-grade students in Seattle, found that 11 percent of the males in their study reported owning a handgun; 6 percent had carried a gun to school sometime in the past. In a related study of young male delinquents (fifteen–eighteen years of age) in a detention center in Seattle, the same research team found that 59 percent of their respondents had owned a handgun and that 70 percent of the gun owners had carried one to school (Callahan, Rivara, and Farrow 1993). Two of every three handgun owners and one of every two members of the whole sample reported shooting at another person.

Finally, Webster, Gainer, and Champion (1993) have reported recently that one in four of the male students they surveyed in two Washington, D.C., public junior high schools had carried a gun for protection or use in a fight. Among the subsample of gun possessors, 16 percent had carried the firearm on more than seven days of the prior two weeks.

Seeking Causes: Guns, Drugs, and Gangs

The Committee on the Judiciary of the U.S. Senate argues in its majority report, *Murder Toll: Initial Projections*, that the causes of the recent increases in violence in America are indisputable:

[W]e need look no further than the "three Ds": drugs, and the mayhem caused by hard-core drug addicts and dealers; deadly weapons, particularly the easily available military-style assault weapons; and demographics, fueling a growth in violent teenaged gangs. (1991:1)

While factors other than those cited by the Committee on the Judiciary surely influence the rates of violence in American cities, the Committee is not alone in its emphasis on guns, drugs, and gangs. Indeed, most popular discussions of gun-related violence by youth have emphasized the connection with drugs and gangs (Eskin 1989; Popkin 1991; Reinhold 1988; *U.S. News and World Report* 1993). School administrators increasingly worry about these phenomena (Stephens 1989). Popular sentiment generally points to drugs, mainly crack cocaine, as an especially corrosive influence that may precipitate considerable gun-related conflict both inside and outside schools (Treaster and Taylor 1992; *Washington Post* 1992; Wolff 1990). As well, emphasis on criminal activity traditionally has been a staple, though not the sole focus of research on gangs (Thrasher 1936; Miller 1958; Short and Strodtbeck 1965). The emphasis remains, though the criminal activity of interest is increasingly violent (Horowitz 1983; Jankowski 1991). Gang violence and gang-related drug trafficking are believed to have risen in recent years in a number of large cities and in many middle-sized and smaller cities and suburban communities as well (Spergel, Chance, and Curry 1990). "[Recent] research suggests higher levels of violence, greater numbers and sophistication of weaponry, broader age ranges . . . and increasing involvement of gang members in drug distribution systems" (Maxson and Klein 1990:71–72). The apparently large profits to be made in the drug trade provide both the reason for violence and the means and motive to procure the most sophisticated and lethal small-arms technology available.

Research Issues

Popular impressions notwithstanding, the available research evidence concerning guns and violence leaves many important questions unanswered. The single largest study of criminal weapons acquisition and use to date centers on *adults* (Wright and Rossi 1986). Similarly, though much anticrime policy discussion focuses on keeping firearms out of the hands of youth, Kleck's (1991) encyclopedic review of gun control research through the 1990s contains no chapter or section devoted to juveniles and has no listing in the index under juveniles, adolescents, teenagers, or youth. Though a number of studies cited above address the issue of the distribution of weapons (not always firearms) among juveniles, we are left nonetheless with an incomplete picture of how many adolescents own, carry, and use firearms, especially on a *routine* basis.

If guns are indeed prevalent among youth, what kinds of guns are they? Much emphasis has been placed in recent years on the so-called military-style weapons, the automatic and semiautomatic rifles that were popularized in several graphic movies of the 1980s and early 1990s. How many juvenile criminals (or, for that matter, inner-city high school students) have owned such a gun? Where and how do juveniles obtain these or other types of firearms? How easily and at what cost? Again, there is a popular impression that guns of all sorts are widely and routinely available to youth, that any fifteen-year-old can obtain a gun with only a modest investment of effort and money. Can it really be that easy? Federal law prohibits juveniles from legally purchasing guns. By what means is the law circumvented?

Many explanations have been advanced for the rising tide of school-related violence, among them the recurring struggle over power and control of the schools between students and teachers (David and Siegenthaler 1985), and the negative labeling of "disruptive" students and subsequent engendering of secondary deviance (Rich 1981, 1982). It is of interest that none of the most commonly offered theories of school violence direct any attention at all to the means and sources of weapons acquisition as a necessary precondition. It seems simply to be *assumed* that any juvenile who wishes to be armed will find the means to do so. How they actually go about it is therefore rarely discussed, although a moment's reflection will confirm that this must lie at the very heart of the problem. As well, relatively little of the research on the topic of guns in schools has focused specifically on *inner-city* schools, where the problem of school violence seems most widespread. How prevalent is gun possession, carrying, and use among students in these institutions?

Where do adolescents get their guns? A recent review of the literature on drugs and gangs (Spergel 1990) notes the increasing violence perpetrated by drug gangs, the utter viciousness of many gang members, and the prevalence of serious weaponry ("AK 47s, 357 magnums, Uzis," p. 190), but as to how this all came to be notes only that gangs have more and better weapons. Juveniles, whether or not gang members, must obtain their weapons from somewhere or somebody; cash or other goods must be exchanged; a system of commerce must exist. Are the guns available to youth primarily stolen from the homes and cars of legitimate firearms owners? If not, then where are they procured?

To what ends are guns possessed and carried? What empirical relationships can be discerned between firearm-related behaviors and involvement in crime, or in the drug trade, or in gangs? How much of what we believe to be true about gangs, drugs, and guns can be substantiated and how much is modern urban myth? What is the motivation for a young person to acquire and carry firearms? Do youth acquire guns mainly for offensive or defensive purposes? And how are the firearms of the young actually used: to commit crimes, to achieve status, to intimidate victims, to protect oneself in a hostile and violent setting?

The number of such questions that can be raised instantly points to a need for information that is not presently available. The same array of unanswered questions suggests, as well, that we do not yet know nearly enough about how, where, and why juveniles obtain and carry guns to design policies that would get them to stop it.

The Present Study

In this book we report the results of research funded by the National Institute of Justice and the Office of Juvenile Justice and Delinquency Prevention and designed to provide answers to many of the questions posed above. Through collection of extensive survey data from two groups of young males—incarcerated juveniles and inner-city high school students—we have sought to address issues that previously have not been researched in depth. We have concentrated our efforts on incarcerated (thus criminally active) juveniles and inner-city youth because these are precisely the youth popularly considered to engage in and experience violence (especially gun-related violence), to belong to the urban street gangs, and to participate in the drug trafficking thought to lead to intense gun violence.[3]

Specifically, our book addresses the following topics:

- respondents' exposure to guns, crime, and violence,
- respondents' criminal activities,
- respondents' drug activity profiles,
- respondents' gang membership profiles,
- gun possession and carrying patterns, including types of guns owned,
- important features of respondents' handguns,
- methods and cost of obtaining guns,
- reasons for carrying guns and situations in which guns are fired,
- gun sales by respondents,
- drug use and sales, crime, and gun activity, and
- gangs, guns, and criminal activity.

Chapter 2 describes the methodology employed in this research. Chapter 3 focuses upon the distribution of guns among juveniles as well as the sources of the guns. Motivations for obtaining guns are considered in Chapter 4. The relationships of drug activity and gang activity to gun-related behavior are explored in Chapters 5 and 6, respectively. Chapter 7 explores three themes related to the issue of "kids and guns": firearms in the hands of female inner-city juveniles, factors associated with weapon-related victimization, and the extent to which firearm-related activity characterizes suburban youth.[4] The final chapter examines the policy implications of the various findings discussed in this book.

Notes

1.   Especially frightening is the possibility that the such experiences become so routine that they no longer have any effect at all. Consider the following account of a colleague who has befriended a twelve-year-old girl from the housing projects of New Orleans. During a recent outing, the girl and our colleague happened upon a murder scene at a busy intersection. Off to the side of the road, police and medical technicians were zipping up a body bag. The twelve-year-old expressed no curiosity about the body bag or its contents. There was no expression of horror or fright, no apparent anxiety or concern. She said simply: "Well, look at that. Some fool got hisself killed," and went back to eating her ice cream cone. Had the girl ever seen a dead person before? "Oh yeah, lots of times." Had she, personally, ever actually seen someone being shot? "Sure!" What did she do when gunshots rang out in the project? "We jump in the closet and shut the door." How often did that happen? "All the time." Had stray rounds ever ended up inside the apartment? "Last weekend."

2.   More often than not, the rate of victimization for this category is the highest of any of the numerous categories employed in the report. When it is not, it is second only to the twenty–twenty-four age category.

3.   We especially feel that to ignore incarcerated juveniles because they represent a select sample both by virtue of their extreme behavior and the fact that they "got caught" is tantamount to ignoring the source of much of the gunplay and violence about which this study is interested. These youth likely are responsible for a very high percentage of the serious crime committed by juveniles, and are far more criminal than the most criminal of nonincarcerated youth (see Cernkovich, Giordano, and Pugh 1985). They were apprehended and incarcerated because they committed so many serious crimes that the odds finally caught up with them.

4.   The discussion of guns in the hands of suburban youth relies on exploratory data collected after the data for the inner-city and serious offender respondents were gathered (see Chapter 7).

2

ASKING DIRECTLY:
THE 1991 YOUTH GUN SURVEY

The aim of quantity in science is not mere maximum precision,
but approximations reliable enough to argue from.
—Philip Morrison, "Book Review," *Scientific American*

Both sampling and the manner of obtaining information from youth about their acquisition, possession, and use of firearms are problematic for researchers. What kinds of research sites should be chosen and what types of youth in them should be studied? How are respondents to be found? One might venture onto urban streets and down back alleys to survey juveniles who could as easily respond with a gun as with an answer. Surveys of more captive respondents by nature are safer, but invariably some portion of the population of interest is not within such groups. Does their loss matter? If the researcher focuses upon incarcerated and inner-city high school youth—as we have done—how are reasonable samples of such juveniles possible? As importantly, how much detail about gun acquisition, possession, and use can be elicited from the young respondents in these select populations?

These issues inform the present chapter. The findings and analyses reported in this book derive from responses to self-administered questionnaires completed by 835 male inmates in six correctional facilities and 758 male students[1] in ten inner-city high schools in the United States. The institutions and schools were located in four states. Work began on the project in September 1990; questionnaires were developed, pretested, and refined in October and November. Negotiations with correctional facilities and school administrators occurred between November 1990, and February 1991. Data collection took place during January through April 1991.

The survey was introduced to students and to inmates as a national study of firearms and violence among youth. Respondents were told that we sought information about what they knew about guns in their neighborhoods and peer groups as well as information about their personal knowledge and experience. In all cases, students and inmates were assured that their participation in the study was voluntary and anonymous.

Research Sites

Absent the resources for a fully national, random sample of research sites, our site selection strategy was highly purposive. We wanted to target areas in which gun-related activities were considered relatively extensive. We also sought sites that, though providing data technically not generalizable, were not obviously and seriously deviant from most sites. Within a given site, we desired gun-related information from criminally active youth and from inner-city youth. The former could be reached through surveys of inmates in major juvenile correction facilities, the latter through surveys of high school students (ninth- through twelfth-graders) in large, inner-city public schools. Thus, our site selection task required us to gain cooperation from two distinct governmental organizations: corrections systems (usually state operated) and local school districts. Our strategy therefore took the form of gaining entry to a juvenile correction facility within a state and then to schools in a major city near the correctional facility.

Pursuing the above criteria and circumscribed by the denial of simultaneous access to correctional and educational units in some states of interest, we chose as research sites two states with known problems of youth violence and two states with lesser but nonetheless recognizable problems: California, Illinois, Louisiana, and New Jersey. The former two reputedly have serious problems regarding gang activity, primarily in Los Angeles and Chicago, respectively (Klein and Maxson 1989; Spergel 1990). The remaining two are less well known for these features. However, New Orleans, the principal city in Louisiana, consistently has high homicide rates relative to those of other cities in the United States (Federal Bureau of Investigation 1993). New Jersey contains a number of older cities, such as Newark, that have exhibited severe economic difficulties and high levels of crime (Bluestone and Harrison 1982; Federal Bureau of Investigation 1993; Wallace and Rothschild 1988).

Correctional Institutions

Ultimately, we obtained permission to enter six juvenile correction facilities in the selected states—three in California and one each in the remaining states. The incarcerated populations of these institutions varied from 172 to 850. Each was a standard state facility housing serious juvenile offenders. The offenses for which the inmates in these sites were incarcerated ranged from drug trafficking to armed robbery to homicide. All but the New Jersey site were maximum security facilities (completely enclosed, heavily guarded, razor-wired). The New Jersey inmates had offense profiles similar to those in the other facilities. However, the facility was not enclosed and so the ambience was less prisonlike; inmates were monitored instead by constant dormitory and classroom roll calls.

Inner-City Schools

The carrying and use of guns and other weapons by high school students, especially while they are in or on the way to and from school, is a highly controversial matter that could reflect poorly on the administration of the schools in question. Thus, access to appropriate high schools was much more difficult than access to correctional facilities. In all cases, the administrators of the local schools from which we gathered our data consented to our research only on the condition that they, their districts, and their specific schools not be identified in any published version of our results. Respecting these wishes, we note here only that we obtained respondents from ten high schools located in five large, prominent cities proximate to the correctional facilities to which we had access. Schools selected for study within these cities were identified by the district administrators as inner-city schools that had experienced firearms incidents in the recent past and whose students likely had encountered gun-related violence (as victims, perpetrators, or bystanders) out of school. Enrollments in these ten inner-city high schools ranged from 900 to 2,100.

Respondent Representativeness

A number of caveats are in order regarding generalizations from our sample of respondents. Just as the four states we visited were not a probability sample of states, the six reformatories and ten schools in which we conducted our surveys were not probability samples of reformatories and inner-city schools. As expected, responses to the questionnaires showed some variation across reformatories and schools, but reflected no systematic site-to-site patterns; that is, different sites emerged as deviant cases for different items, and no general pattern was discernible in these deviations. Most importantly, site differences most often reduced to a single site at variance with the others. For these reasons, the reporting of site-to-site differences throughout this document would occur in an explanatory vacuum. For the student sample, it would also occur without meaningful identification. In the analyses that follow, therefore, the datasets are treated as two simple cross sections. Site (state in which inmates were incarcerated or the students attended school) is controlled in all multivariate analyses reported in later chapters.

Inmate Sample

While we have reason to believe that respondents within our correctional facilities were "typical," the specific inmates who completed our questionnaires were not chosen randomly; rather, we solicited volunteers and administered the survey to all who came forth. We asked superintendents of the correctional facilities to grant us access to *at least* a quarter of the inmates when we visited their institutions (the number actually surveyed varied from 22 percent of the facility's population to 62 percent, with a mean of 41 percent; percentage surveyed was in large part a function of the size of the facility), and we also stressed that we sought a sample as "representative" as possible (allowing for unique security issues facing each superintendent and emphasizing that, in the end, inmate participation in the study must be voluntary).

In all of the facilities in question, administrators responded by announcing the study to wards in each of the smaller facilities' dormitories and to those in about half of the larger facilities' dormitories. Each ward was offered the opportunity to participate. Those who volunteered were then addressed by us on the day of the survey, listened to our explanation of the research project, and chose to take part in it or to return to their dormitories or classrooms. Beyond this, we sought to maximize response rates by offering five-dollar inducements to participate in the research, by providing Spanish-language versions of the questionnaire to inmates who preferred them, and by conducting personal interviews (covering the entire questionnaire) with inmates whose reading skills were insufficient to complete the questionnaire on their own. The method of distributing the survey to correctional inmates was uniform across sites. In all cases, groups of ten to twenty inmates completed the questionnaire at a time. Average completion time for the survey was about one hour.

Ultimately, then, we missed inmates who were inaccessible for disciplinary or health reasons and those who chose not to participate in the survey. Our interviews with both administrators and inmates suggested that the absentees differed little from the participants. In the one California facility in which data concerning race of residents were made available to us, their perception seemed accurate. Of the 237 inmates housed in the dormitories in which our study was announced, 24 percent were white, 37 percent black, 31 percent hispanic, and 8 percent "other." Of the 144 (61 percent) who volunteered for the project, the corresponding percentages were 24, 36, 34, and 6.

Additionally, comparison of our respondents' profiles with those of inmates in other institutions indicates that ours was a reasonable cross section of inmates—at least those about whom researchers have data. Table 2.1 offers comparisons of our sample of inmates with those of the 1987 *Survey of Youth in Custody* conducted by the Department of Justice (Beck, Kline, and Greenfeld 1988), concerning variables for which data are mutually available. The two populations are not strictly comparable

Table 2.1. Present (1991) Inmate Sample Characteristics vs. Those of Incarcerated Youth in 1987 (*N* Not Reported)[a]

	1987 %	1991 %	(N)
Times incarcerated			(783)
1–2	68	71	
3–6	24	20	
7–10	5	5	
11 +	3	4	
Times arrested			(746)
1–2	28	20	
3–5	29	24	
6–10	21	26	
11+	22	30	

	11–14		15–17		18+		
(By age, years)	1987	1991	1987	1991	1987	1991	
Race							(799)
White[b]	46	38	54	43	55	50	
Black	47	57	40	48	41	42	
Other	7	5	6	9	5	8	
Hispanic	10	14	16	29	31	29	(799)
Grade level							(797)
6th or less	46	39	9	5	4	2	
7th or 8th	51	42	49	27	18	17	
Some high school	3	19	41	67	68	75	
High school	0	0	1	1	10	6	

continued

Table 2.1   (Continued)

(By age, years)	1987 %		1991 %		(N)
	Under 18		18 or older		
	1987	1991	1987	1991	
Prior living situation					(738)
Both parents	28	23	35	16	
Mother only	50	35	44	37	
Father only	6	6	5	9	
Other	16	36	16	38	
Sibling incarcerated	24	47	29	48	(753)
Drug use					
Marijuana	81	84	86	81	(711)
Cocaine	43	47	55	46	(712)
Heroin	12	23	16	22	(712)
First major drug use[c]					(794)
Under 12	14	20	10	15	
12–13	33	26	20	22	
14–17	53	54	64	58	
18+			6	5	

[a] Age categories are those employed by Beck et al.
[b] Includes Hispanics.
[c] For 1987 youth: heroin, cocaine, LSD, PCP. For 1991 sample: "hard" drugs.

since the latter included inmates in all types of state-operated facilities and included a small percentage (7 percent) of females, while ours was composed of more seriously criminal males only. As well, since we are dealing with more serious offenders, we compare in Table 2.2 the race and drug use characteristics of those in our sample eighteen years and older with those of incarcerated male felons of all ages in eleven state prisons who participated in a 1982 study of patterns of adult firearm acquisition and use (Wright and Rossi 1986) and with 1986 known characteristics of male state prison inmates of all ages in the United States (U.S. Department of Justice 1988). Our assumption is that inmates in our sample who were eighteen years of age or older technically could have been serving time in a state prison for adult offenders.

As noted in Table 2.1, our sample was very much like inmates in state youth facilities in number of times incarcerated, though more likely—not surprisingly, given their more serious criminal records—to have been arrested more often. Our sample contained a somewhat lower percentage of white youth and somewhat higher percentages of black and hispanic youth than were found in the average institution. It was also somewhat higher in number of years of schooling, even after controlling for age of respondents. Prior to being incarcerated, our respondents were generally less likely to have lived in some sort of parental household situation and, as befits the seriousness of their crime patterns, more likely to have lived in other arrangements, primarily with friends and on the street, again even after controlling for age.[2] A much higher percentage also came from families in which brothers or sisters had been incarcerated. Involvement in marijuana and cocaine use was roughly the same for both groups, though members of our sample were somewhat more likely to have used heroin. Age at entry into "major" drug use also was roughly the same for both groups.

We found similarities as well, reported in Table 2.2, in comparisons of the race and ethnic and drug use characteristics of wards in our sample who were at least eighteen years old with those of the incarcerated adult felon sample from the 1982 study and those of males in state prisons in 1986. The race/ethnicity profiles of all three groups were strikingly similar, although percentage of Hispanics among whites was not uniform across all three groups. Marijuana use was nearly identical across the two groups for whom comparisons were possible; the adult felons were more likely to have used both cocaine and heroin.

In sum, we did not seek a purely random sample of inmates from the institutions we visited. However, our respondents displayed much the same characteristics as did inmates in similar settings. Our sample, drawn purposely to maximize our information about gun-related activ-

Table 2.2. 1990 Inmate Sample, 18 Years and Older, vs. 1982 Adult Felons[a] and 1986 Inmates in State Prisons[b] Concerning Race/Ethnicity and Drug Characteristics

	1982 Felons		1986 Prisoners		1990 Sample	
	%	(N)	%	(N)	%	(N)
Race		(*)		(13,573)		(115)
White	50		52		50	
Black	40		45		42	
Other	10		3		8	
Hispanic	7	(*)	13	(13,025)	14	(115)
Drug use						
Marijuana	84	(1648)	[Data not		81	(105)
Cocaine	56	(1622)	available]		46	(101)
Heroin	34	(1614)			22	(103)

[a] Wright and Rossi (1986).
[b] U.S. Department of Justice.
[*] N not provided.

ities, was clearly not an unusual or atypical cross section of youth incarcerated in maximum-security settings.

Student Sample

Selection of respondents from among the high school population for this study proceeded along the same lines and posed essentially the same problems as did sampling among the inmate population. Principals were asked to grant us access to 150 to 200 students in each of the schools we entered and, within the practical constraints faced by principals and teachers, to make the sample—students in grades nine through twelve—as representative of their students as possible. In six instances, principals arranged for the survey to take place during homeroom periods. These periods were uniform for the student body; thus, theoretically, we had access to the entire student population. In two schools, the survey was given during the physical education hours, and in two schools we were granted access to all students enrolled in social studies courses. In the former two sites, physical education was mandatory and its hours were uniform for all students; thus, here too, theoretically, we had access to all students. In the two sites in which we entered social studies courses, our access to the entire student body was more limited.

In some schools, the survey was administered to groups of twenty to thirty students at a time. In others, it was given to larger assemblies of 100 to 200 students. Method of distribution did not influence responses to the questionnaire items. In four schools, principals permitted us to offer a five-dollar inducement to students to participate in the study. While this reward, or its absence, may have influenced the percentage of students who volunteered for the study, it was not tied to variation in the percentage of students surveyed across schools (in fact, the highest participation rates derived from schools without financial incentives). Nor was there any relationship between responses to questionnaire items and whether or not students were rewarded for their participation. As with the inmate study, we offered Spanish-language versions of the questionnaire to students who preferred them.

The number of students surveyed in each school ranged from 109 to 229 (with a mean of 165). Percentage of student populations surveyed across schools ranged from 7 to 21 (with a mean of 10 percent; as with the inmate survey, lower percentages were a function of larger-size schools). Since our selection of schools was not random, since participation in the study was voluntary, and since we had no access to students absent on the day of the survey, we cannot claim that the students we questioned were representative of inner-city students generally nor necessarily representative of stu-

Table 2.3. Present Student Sample Characterisitics vs. Those of a Sample of Inner-City Students from Four Cities[a]

	Four-cities sample		Present sample	
	%	(N)[b]	%	(N)[b]
Race/ethnicity		(403)		(756)
White	2		3	
Black	65		72	
Hispanic	26		19	
Other	7		6	
Age		(403)		(753)
14	11		7	
15	25		24	
16	25		27	
17	21		23	
18+	18		19	
Single-parent home	56	(403)	45	(752)
Used hard drugs[c]	6	(403)	6	(574)
Used alcohol	22	(403)	58	(741)
Sold drugs	5	(403)	18	(560)
Victim of violence[d]	50	(403)	30	(583)

[a] *Source:* Fagan et al. (1986), Fagan et al. (1987).
[b] Missing cases not noted.
[c] For four-cities study: heroin, cocaine, PCP, barbiturates, amphetamines. For the present study: heroin, cocaine, barbituates, amphetamines.
[d] For four-cities study: roberry by force or threat of force, attack with a weapon, beating, or threat of beating. For the present study: shot at, stabbed with a knife, injured with some other weapon.

dents in the schools we visited. However, principals and teachers indicated that they considered them representative of their students. As a limited check on this perception, we had ascertained from the schools, prior to administration of our survey, estimates of the racial and ethnic distribution of their students. In all instances, distributions within our samples fell within 4 percent of those of the larger populations.

As well, a 1984 study of inner-city high school students' criminal behavior permits a limited assessment of comparability concerning selected characteristics. In that study of violent delinquency, Fagan, Piper, and Moore (1986) and Fagan, Piper, and Cheng (1987) employed data collected from randomly selected high school students from inner-city, high-crime neighborhoods in the Bronx, Dallas, Miami, and Chicago. As the comparisons with the present sample in Table 2.3 indicate, age and race breakdowns for the two samples are similar. A lower percentage of our respondents lived in single-parent households.[3] Use of the drugs of interest to Fagan and his colleagues was the same for both samples though the present sample was considerably more likely to have sold drugs.[4] Alcohol use was also much higher in the present sample. Finally, using a more liberal measure of violent victimization (including both use of force and threat of use of force), Fagan et al. report that 50 percent of their sample had been victimized in the past year. Our respondents were asked more narrowly whether they had been shot at with a gun, stabbed with a knife, or injured with some other weapon in the past few years. Thirty percent had been so victimized.

The behavioral discrepancies between the two samples may result from our use of students from specifically identified "problem" *schools* as opposed to the use by Fagan et al. of randomly sampled students in schools in "problem" *neighborhoods*. That is, even in high-problem neighborhoods, less problematic schools may have produced a less criminal sample. The difference in victimization rate likely would disappear with more similar measurement. In sum, based on limited comparative data, our respondents appear similar sociodemographically to inner-city students sampled in other studies. However, because we sought schools known to have had weapons problems, our average respondent appears more criminally involved than the average inner-city student.[5]

Finally, we reemphasize that we have focused our attention exclusively on inner-city public schools with well-publicized violence problems. Not all inner-city public schools are as troubled as the ten in which we surveyed students. As important, nothing in our data reflects the situation in suburban or rural high schools. If media and some scholarly accounts are correct, the problems of gangs, drugs, guns, and violence have begun to spread outward from the central cities and into the suburban fringe (e.g., Spergel, Chance, and Curry 1990). Our data say nothing about these developments, nor do they speak to the situation of urban private, parochial, or elite public high schools. Research that extends our results to the suburban and rural areas would be useful (see Chapter 7).

Missing Data

Yet another element of the issue of representativeness concerns missing data on individual items throughout the questionnaire. Considerable missing data were expected given that ours was a long survey, that time limits were imposed on some groups of respondents (especially students in courses), and that we had told respondents that answering any given item in the survey was discretionary. Analysis of the missing data in the present study suggests that most stem from time constraints. That is, the vast majority of incomplete items occurred at the end of the survey, and these were more characteristic of respondents, particularly students, who had to leave the survey setting at a given time for another class. For the inmate sample (generally with more time allotted for questionnaire completion), missing cases averaged 7.8 percent across items, within a range of 2.3 to 16.5 percent. Students averaged 13.9 percent within a range of 3.2 to 29.3 percent. Randomly cross-tabulating any two items that appeared in the first two-thirds of the questionnaire, we found little in the way of systematic nonresponse (as opposed to that associated with incomplete items in the last third of the survey due to time limitation). Average percentage of inmate respondents who failed to complete both items in any set was 1.41 within a range of 0.11 (literally, one case) to 4.1 percent. The average for students was 3.1 percent within a range of 0.7 to 3.9 percent.

Throughout this book the number of cases varies across items and, when items are cross-tabulated (especially items from the last third of the survey), the number of missing cases can grow quite large. The primary issue in this regard is whether those who responded to items differed from those who did not. Thus, for both inmates and students, we compared missing cases on a number of items (gun possession, drug activity, victimization, criminality) against responding cases controlling for age, race/ethnicity, and grade level. For both samples, missing and responding cases differed little in terms of age and grade-level profiles. However, race and ethnicity did enter into the picture for both samples regarding all but, importantly, gun possession items. Among inmates, missing cases for drug-related and victimization items were more likely to be Hispanic than were responding cases. Missing cases for items tapping use of weapons in crimes more likely pertained to black respondents than did responding cases. Among students, blacks were more highly represented among missing cases for drug-related and victimization items; no differences were found for items regarding criminal activity with weapons. Given that prior research has found that blacks tend to underreport criminal activity in self-report surveys (Huizinga and Elliott 1986; Hindelang, Hirschi, and Weis 1981), these findings were not unexpected. They also prompted a further important check on missing data whereby we replicated the analyses reported below substituting predicted values for all missing cases (Anderson, Basilevsky, and Hum 1983). The results were substantially unchanged.

Methodological Issues

Survey Items

The research questionnaires employed in this study covered roughly the same core topics for both inmates and students. Items were primarily forced-choice. They dealt with sociodemographic characteristics, school experiences, gun ownership, gun use (for several types of fire-arms), gun acquisition patterns, gun-carrying habits, use of other weapons, gang membership and gang activities, self-reported criminality and criminal justice record, victimization patterns, drug and alcohol use, and attitudes concerning guns, crime, and violence. In both questionnaires, the majority of items dealt with firearms knowledge, acquisition, and use. The remaining items in the inmate survey were devoted primarily to criminal behavior and secondarily to victimization histories; in the student survey, these priorities were reversed. This translates to missing cells regarding student criminality items in many tables to follow. In the coming pages, specific measurements derived from the questionnaire items are described on a topic-by-topic basis.

Reliability and Validity

Self-reported criminality always has been a two-edged sword for researchers. On the one hand, this form of data is absolutely necessary to the study of most types of deviance. Official data simply do not provide the level of information appropriate to attempts to link, for example, drug-related activity and ownership of automatic weapons. On the other hand, beyond technical concerns with such matters as preferred-offense items, response categories, and time-frame (see Elliott and Ageton 1980; Jensen and Rojek 1980), issues of reliability and validity cast large shadows upon self-reported criminality investigations.

However, self-reported criminality data probably suffer less from problems of reliability and validity than most observers would guess (Horney and Marshall 1992). Using polygraph tests, for example, Clark and Tifft (1966) found most responses by juveniles to self-report items truthful (see also Akers, Massey, Clarke, and Lauer 1983). Researchers have found that few respondents who report no offenses have police records (Elliott and Voss 1974; Hardt and Peterson-Hardt 1977; Hirschi 1969). Others have established that self-report data generally are free of dishonesty by questioning the respondents' peers and teachers about the veracity of their statements. Farrington (1973) noted that 75 percent of the self-reported delinquency in one study was re-reported in a second study two years later. Indeed, systematic reviews of the literature generally have accorded self-reported criminality data fairly high marks (O'Brien 1985). As Hindelang, Hirschi, and Weis commented: "Reliability measures are impressive and the majority of studies produce validity coefficients in the moderate to strong range" (1981:114). To the extent that problems have arisen, they have indicated that more seriously criminal respondents are more subject to memory lapses and telescoping of their reports. Data from black respondents also may be less reliable and valid than those from white respondents (Huizinga and

Elliott 1986), and females and males may respond unevenly to prevalence questions (Sampson 1985).

Our attempts to establish levels of reliability and validity in the present study centered on responses to a number of items. In each instance, responses to a pair of items were checked for logical consistency. For example, respondents who claimed never to have owned a military-style weapon at any time in their lives should not have responded affirmatively to a later item regarding ownership of such a weapon just prior to incarceration (for the inmates) or at the present time (for the students). Fourteen such items were examined for the inmates. Percentage of inconsistent answers ranged from 1.2 to 3.4; average percentage of inconsistency was 2.4. Eleven items were examined for the student sample. Inconsistent responses averaged 1.5 percent within a range of 0.7 to 3.1 percent. To determine how systematic were the inconsistencies, we scored each respondent on number of inconsistent answers. Among the inmates, each of whom received an inconsistency score between 0 and 14, only 4 percent scored above 2; no one scored above 6 (one case only at 6). Students received a score between 0 and 11. Only 1 percent scored above 2; no score exceeded 4.

Beyond the consistency check, validity becomes difficult to assess, since we have no official records against which to compare our self-report data. Our analysis of missing cases suggested a lower validity level for black inmates (via underreporting of criminal offenses) though not for black students (see above). Generally, however, validity in studies like this one must rely primarily upon degree of correlation regarding measures concerning apparently similar attitudes and behaviors (also a measure of reliability) and correlations between variables known to be related through prior research.

Our examination of such relationships suggests a reasonably high level of validity for both samples. For example, respondents who attributed respect from peers to ownership of a gun also felt that friends would look down on them if they did not carry a gun (Pearson's $r = .638$ for inmates, .587 for students). Regarding relationships found in prior research, we have focused on drug-use patterns. For both samples, level of use of heroin, crack, and regular cocaine was associated with extent of commission of property crimes to gain drug money (for inmates, r ranges between .245 and .384; for students, r ranges between .395 and .453)—a finding consistent with those of previous researchers (Chaiken and Chaiken 1990:212). Among the students, heroin, crack, and regular cocaine use were very highly correlated (r between any two exceeds .820); for inmates, the relationship was milder ($r = .320$ through .527). In either case, the tendency toward polydrug use by heavy users of any type of drug has been reported in other research (Elliott, Huizinga, and Menard 1989; Wish and Johnson 1986). In sum, reliability and validity levels for both samples seem to exceed what might be expected for respondents of the type surveyed in the present study and for the subject matter of interest here. Though it is easy to imagine respondents treating our survey less than seriously, it seems, quite to the contrary, that frivolous and inaccurate responses were relatively infrequent.

Respondent Sociodemographic Characteristics

Inmate Sample

Table 2.4 presents descriptive data on the social and demographic characteristics of our institutionalized respondents. Since all but one of

Table 2.4. Sociodemographic Characteristics of Incarcerated and Student Samples

Characteristics	Inmates		Students	
	%	(N)	%	(N)
Age		(814)		(753)
<15	3		7	
15	9		24	
16	20		27	
17	27		23	
18	27		16	
19+	14		3	
Race/ethnicity		(821)		(756)
White	16		3	
Black	46		72	
Hispanic	29		19	
Asian	3		5	
Other	6		1	
Education (grade)		(799)		(747)
6th or less	4			
7th or 8th	24			
9th	25		25	
10th	27		32	
11th	18		21	
12th	2		22	
Size of city of residence		(702)		(758)
<50,000	20			
50,000–100,000	11			
100,001–250,000	13			
250,001–500,000	29		26	
500,001+	27		74	

these institutions were maximum-security facilities, the age distribution of the respondents, not surprisingly, is skewed toward the upper end of the spectrum (mean = 17 years). Blacks comprised nearly half (46 percent) of the inmate sample; Hispanics comprised 29 percent (possibly misleading since three of the six facilities were in California). Whites made up only 16 percent of the sample; Asians and others comprised the remaining 9 percent. Twenty-eight percent of the sample had no more than an eighth-grade education; the modal educational attainment was tenth grade; practically none had completed a high school degree. Most inmates were from cities of at least 250,000 residents. Thus, ours was a sample largely of young, nonwhite, undereducated, inner-city males.

Student Sample

Table 2.4 also provides the sociodemographic profile of our high school respondents. The sample was 72 percent black; only 3 percent of the students were white. The Hispanic and Asian portions of the sample (19 and 5 percent, respectively) were found predominantly in the California schools. Most students were between fifteen and seventeen years old (mean age = 16); the modal grade level was tenth.

The relative socioeconomic homogeneity of our two samples precludes much in the way of differences across sociodemographic lines regarding the behaviors presently of interest. However, in Chapter 3, we explore the relationship of firearms ownership and carrying to site and pertinent sociodemographic variables, and in succeeding chapters we control for these and other variables in multivariate analyses.

Sociocriminal Profiles

Hostile Environment

Prior to examining the gun-related behaviors of our respondents, it is important to place those behaviors in a larger social context. Most people perceive the social worlds of youth as increasingly violent and hostile. However, the magnitude of the problem as it is experienced by persons like our respondents may surpass common perceptions. Much that appears aberrant or deviant when assessed against a middle-class standard has become in fact a commonplace feature of life for many of them.

Table 2.5 presents data on the exposure of both our samples to guns, crime, and violence in their family, peer, and neighborhood contexts.[6] Among the incarcerated juveniles, a third reported siblings who had committed "serious" (unspecified) crimes; two in ten had siblings who

Table 2.5.   Exposure to Guns, Crime, and Violence—Inmates and Students[a]

	Inmates		Students	
	%	(N)	%	(N)
Sibling records (% yes)				
Committed "serious" crime	35	(800)	12	(723)
Arrested	55	(799)	*	
Incarcerated	42	(800)	*	
Guns in the family (% yes)				
Handguns in home	*		37	(555)
Siblings own guns	47	(794)	*	
Siblings own handguns	*		28	(710)
Males in family own guns	79	(754)	69	(692)
Males in family carry guns	62	(730)	37	(692)
Friends and guns (% yes)				
Friends own guns	90	(763)	57	(692)
Friends carry guns	89	(728)	42	(684)
Respondent's victimization history (% yes)				
Threatened with gun or shot at	84	(731)	45	(697)
Stabbed with a knife	50	(729)	*	
stabbed with a knife in or on way to school	*		10	(591)
Beaten up	82	(728)	*	
Beaten up in or on way to school	*		30	(591)
Injured with weapon (not knife or gun) in or on way to school	*		17	(590)

[a] Measurement described in text.
* Item not included in this sample's survey.

had been arrested for a crime; four in ten inmates had siblings who had been incarcerated. Forty-seven percent had siblings who owned guns. More generally, 79 percent of the inmates came from families in which at least some of the males owned guns. Sixty-two percent had male family members who *carried* guns routinely outside the home. Among fathers, siblings, and other male family members, in short, most of our inmate respondents grew up in families where firearms were routinely present and where gun carrying was apparently the norm.

The pattern is even sharper concerning the peers of the incarcerated juveniles. Ninety percent of the inmates had at least some friends and associates who owned and carried guns routinely. Thus, in the street environment inhabited by these juvenile offenders, owning and carrying guns were virtually universal behaviors—not an aberration characteristic of only a few but a normative and widespread standard. Further, in this same environment, our inmate respondents regularly experi-

enced threats of violence and violence itself. Eighty-four percent reported that they themselves had been threatened with a gun or shot at
during their lives.[7] Half had been stabbed with a knife. More than eight
in ten (82 percent) had been beaten.

If the social world of the student respondents seems less dangerous
or hostile, it is only by comparison to that of the inmates. Twelve percent
of the students reported siblings who had committed serious crimes.
Seven out of ten students said there were males in their families who
owned guns; *handguns* were present in 37 percent of the homes. [In the
nation as a whole, about half of all households possess a firearm of some
sort, and handguns are present in approximately a quarter (Wright,
Rossi, and Daly 1983; Kleck 1991)]. Sixty-nine percent had males in their
families who owned guns. Two-fifths of the students reported that
males in their families carried guns routinely outside the home.

Gun owning and carrying were also common among the friends and
peers of our student sample. More than half (57 percent) of our respondents had friends who owned guns; 42 percent had friends who carried
guns routinely outside the home. Like members of the inmate sample,
the student respondents also were frequently threatened and victimized
by violence. Forty-five percent had been threatened with a gun or shot at
while on the way to or from school in the last few years. One in ten had
been stabbed, and one in three beaten up in or on the way to school.
Nearly a fifth (17 percent) had been wounded with some form of weapon other than a knife or a gun in or near the school.

Victimization aside, our data also permit some comment concerning
violence in the inner-city schools in which we surveyed students. Nearly
a quarter (22 percent) of the students we surveyed reported that the
carrying of weapons to their school was common [i.e., agreed or strongly agreed (as opposed to disagreeing or strongly disagreeing) that "lots
of kids carry weapons to school"]. Nearly half (47 percent) personally
knew schoolmates at whom shots had been fired in the last few years.
Fifteen percent personally knew someone who had carried a weapon to
school; 8 percent personally knew someone who had brought a *gun* to
school. Not surprisingly then, more than a third (35 percent) of the
student respondents agreed or strongly agreed that "there is a lot of
violence in this school." Perhaps indicative of adaptation or resignation
to these obviously dangerous elements, only 14 percent of the respondents described themselves as "scared in school most of the time"—
though one in seven students expressing such fears is hardly trivial.[8]

The reality of violence in the respondents' worlds shapes or is shaped
by their attitudes about violence. We asked both samples a series of
questions about when they felt it was acceptable ("okay") to shoot someone. Response possibilities were strongly disagree, disagree, agree,

strongly agree. Thirty-five percent of the inmates and 10 percent of the students agreed or strongly agreed that "it is okay to shoot a person if that is what it takes to get something you want." Was it "okay to shoot some guy who doesn't belong in your neighborhood?" Twenty-nine percent of the inmates and ten percent of the students agreed or strongly agreed that it was. Elements of insult and injury inevitably increased the perceived acceptance of violent responses. It was considered "okay [agree or strongly agree] to shoot someone who hurts or insults you" by 61 percent of the inmates and 28 percent of the students. If one's family was the target of the insult or injury, the percentage agreeing rose to 74 among the inmates, 24 percent agreeing and 50 percent agreeing strongly.[9]

In general, the students were relatively less accepting of violence than were the inmates. It may be that young people with attitudes that condone violence are more likely to commit violence and therefore end up in juvenile corrections facilities; alternatively, the experience of incarceration itself may cause juveniles to be more accepting of violence as a means of settling interpersonal conflicts. Nonetheless, one out of ten students in our sample found it acceptable to shoot a stranger in his neighborhood or to shoot someone to get something he coveted.

Criminal Histories

A general profile of the criminal histories and activities of youth in the correctional facilities is provided in Table 2.6. (We focus here on non–drug offenses; drug activities are covered in the next section.) Although our average respondent was only seventeen years old, arrest records were lengthy, with more than half the sample having been arrested six or more times. More than a third (36 percent) experienced their first arrest before they were ten years old, and the average age at first arrest was about thirteen. Approximately half had been in a correctional facility at least once prior to their current incarceration; nearly a fourth had experienced their first incarceration prior to age thirteen. Thus, as a whole, these respondents had been arrested and jailed with some frequency. Although still too young, perhaps, to be considered "career criminals," they were at least active apprentices.[10]

We asked respondents whether they had ever committed an armed robbery ("stuck up stores or people") or committed a burglary ("broke into houses, stores, or shops"), regardless of the offense for which they were currently incarcerated. Half had committed a robbery; 65 percent had committed burglary. As well, 38 percent had committed "a property crime specifically because [the respondent] needed money for alcohol or drugs."

By way of comparison to the results for the inmates, our data for the

Table 2.6.   Inmates' Criminal Profiles

	%	(N)
Age at first arrest		(815)
Never arrested	2	
5–9	35	
10–12	13	
13–16	47	
17+	3	
Number of arrests		(761)
None	2	
1–5	42	
6–10	18	
11–15	15	
16–20	7	
21+	11	
Age at first time in correctional facility		(741)
5–9	3	
10–12	23	
13–16	66	
17+	8	
Number of times in correctional facilities		(783)
1 (first time)	51	
2	20	
3	9	
4	6	
5+	14	
Crimes committed (% yes)[a]		
Robbery	49	(811)
Burglary	65	(814)
Property crime for drug money	38	(750)

[a] Measurement described in text.

high school students indicate substantially less criminal activity. Still, 43 percent of the students reported having been "arrested or picked up by the police" at least once; 6 percent had been arrested or picked up "many" times; 23 percent reported having "stolen something worth more than $50." Finally, 6 percent had committed "a property crime specifically because [he] needed money for alcohol or drugs."

Hard Drug Activity

Respondents in both samples were asked the frequency of use of heroin, cocaine, and crack during the "year or two" preceding administration of the survey (for the inmates, during the year or two preceding confinement). As reported in Table 2.7, 43 percent of the inmates had used cocaine, 25 percent crack, and 21 percent heroin. Forty-seven percent reported some use of heroin, cocaine, and crack in the aggregate. Most use of hard drugs occurred no more than "a few times." Use of any individual hard drug was reported by only 5 or 6 percent of the students; use of hard drugs in the aggregate was reported by only 7 percent of the students (again, most use was confined to "a few times").[11]

Table 2.7 also presents distributions regarding a *hard-drug use score*. Hard-drug use was measured by combining responses concerning use of each of the three substances in question: heroin, cocaine, and crack. A respondent might have used each "never" (scored 0), "once" (scored 1), "only a few times" (scored 2), "many times" (scored 3), or "almost all the time" (scored 4) in the year or two preceding confinement. Summing responses to these items produces a hard-drug use score that can range from 0 to 12 (used all three substances "almost all the time"). Thirteen percent of the inmates had hard-drug use scores of no more than 2 (two drugs once each or one drug "a few times"). Thirty-four percent had scores of 3 or higher.

Due to the attention in the literature to potentially differential criminal involvement across *types* of "heavy" drug users (Gentry 1995), we also have typed such users in our samples (those who used heroin, cocaine, or crack, individually or in combination, "many times" or "almost all the time" during the past year or two) into four categories: heroin users only, cocaine users only, crack users only, and polydrug users only (used at least two of the three drug types). The last of these does not include members of the first three categories. As the findings in Table 2.7 indicate, the inmate sample included 183 "heavy" drug users (25 percent of the sample), 40 percent of whom were cocaine and 39 percent of whom were polydrug users; among the students were 31 "heavy" drug users (5 percent of the sample), 71 percent of whom were polydrug users.

A third of the inmates (but only 4 percent of the students) had been in alcohol or drug treatment programs. Often, such programs are mandatory for users upon admission to a correctional facility. They also may have been requirements of earlier probation sentences imposed by the juvenile courts.

Finally, respondents were asked which of the following best described their involvement in drug sales: (a) never used or sold drugs, (b) was a user only, (c) was a dealer myself, (d) worked for a dealer, and (e) was both a user and a dealer. Those who chose response (c), (d), or (e) were classified as dealers for the purposes of this study. Seventy-three percent of the inmates had sold drugs (48 percent had sold but not

Table 2.7 Respondents' Drug Involvement[a]

Item[b]	Inmates		Students	
	%	(N)	%	(N)
Frequency of use				
Heroin		(716)		(579)
Never	79		96	
Few times or less	12		3	
Many times	5		0.8	
Almost all the time	4		0.2	
Regular cocaine		(717)		(579)
Never	57		94	
Few times or less	21		3	
Many times	11		1	
Almost all the time	11		2	
Crack cocaine		(721)		(582)
Never	75		95	
Few times or less	13		2	
Many times	5		1	
Almost all the time	7		2	
Use of any of heroin, cocaine, or crack	47	(689)	7	(586)
Hard-drug score[c]		(719)		(576)
0	53		93	
1	3		1	
2	10		1	
3	7		0.5	
4 or more	27		4.5	
"Heavy" drug users[d]	25	(725)	5	(581)
Ever in alcohol or drug treatment program?		(751)		(592)
Never	64		96	
Once	20		2	
Few times	12		1	
Many times	4		1	
Drug sales[b]	72	(695)	18	(581)
Sales only	47		16	
Use and sales	25		2	

[a] Year or two immediately preceding incarceration for inmates; past year or two for students.
[b] Measurement described in text.
[c] Sum of the frequency scores for each of the three drugs; range = 0–12.
[d] Use of any or a combination of heroin, cocaine, or crack "many times" or "almost all the time" in the previous year or two.

used drugs; 25 percent had both used and sold drugs). Eighteen percent of the students had sold drugs (16 percent had sold but not used drugs; 2 percent had both used and sold drugs).

Gang Membership

As noted earlier, the notion of a link between gangs and gun-related violence is common in most discussions of crime in the nation's urban centers, yet researchers in this area have found definitions and typologies of gangs hard to construct. Whether definitions should include the criminal behavior whose explanation is the object of the defining or typing is problematic (Morash 1983). As well, some observers debate distinctions between gangs and delinquent groups (Morash 1983; Spergel 1990:179–80). Conventional wisdom suggests such a distinction, assigning a looseness and transiency of organization and activity to delinquent groups and defining gang activity thus:

> [L]aw-violating behavior committed by juveniles or adults in or related to groups that are complexly organized although sometimes diffuse, sometimes cohesive with established leadership and rules. The gang also engages in a range of crime but significantly more violence [than mere delinquent groups] within a framework of communal values in respect to mutual support, conflict relations with other gangs, and a tradition often of turf, colors, signs, and symbols. (Curry and Spergel 1988:382; see also Klein and Maxson 1989:212)

While the above definition permits distinctions between delinquent groups and gangs, it does not emphasize differences among gangs in their structural features and activities. Expanding the definition then, we argue first that gangs should be defined as such by their members. Second, they should possess, though differentially, such organizational features as a name, designated leadership, turf, colors, and regular "meetings." Whether or not these elements are linked to criminal behavior—firearms activity in the present study—is the topic of our inquiry.

In the present study, respondents were asked if, in the past year or two (for the inmates, prior to confinement), they belonged to a "gang" and, if so, whether or not it was organized and possessed a number of characteristics. These included size of the gang and attributes normally associated with gangs—an "official" name, designated leadership, regular meetings, designated clothing, and a specified turf to be defended (Curry and Spergel 1988; Fagan 1989). "Gangness," as opposed to "groupness," was determined by the respondent's designation of his gang as "organized" or as "just a bunch of people." Gang size was collapsed into two categories, one above and the other at or below the mean (50 for the inmates, 10 for the students). A gang attribute score ranging from 0 to 5 was calculated via the sum of responses to the five above-named gang characteristics. Latent class analysis of the cross-classification of these three variables (Lazarsfeld and Henry 1968; Clogg 1981) found them adequately described by a two-class model ($L^2 = 15.78$, $\chi^2 = 12.5$, df = 8 for the inmate gang members; $L^2 = 13.37$, $\chi^2 = 13.2$, df = 8 for the student gang members). The resulting classes could be characterized substantively as "structured" vs. "unstructured" gangs. Fifty-nine percent of the inmates belonged to gangs: 74 percent of these were affiliated with structured gangs and 26 percent with unstructured gangs. Twenty-two percent of the students claimed gang affiliation: 39 percent of these with structured and 61 percent with unstructured gangs. Structured gangs were characterized by high conditional probabilities of having fifty or more members among inmates and ten or more among students, of being called "organized" by their members, and of having a gang attribute score of 3 or higher for inmates and 2 or higher for students.

Having examined the sociodemographic and sociocriminal profiles of the profiles of our respondents, we turn in Chapter 3 to the focus of the present study: gun acquisition, possession, and sale among adolescents.

Notes

1. Data were also collected from female students in these schools, but the percentage of these respondents engaging in gun-related activities was sufficiently limited that little would be gained by introducing the gender variable into a study already complicated by a focus on different samples of males. Summary results regarding female firearm-related behavior are reported in Chapter 7.

2. Only a quarter of the inmates (26 percent) lived with both parents prior to their current incarceration. A plurality (33 percent) lived with mothers only (that is, in female-headed households); a fifth lived with fathers (3 percent) or other relatives (17 percent); and the remainder were dispersed across a variety of living situations, including some who were living in the streets (that is, were homeless) and some who were living in foster care arrangements. On average, our respondents came from large families; the mean number of siblings was 4.2.

3. More of the students than the inmates lived in two-parent households, but the majority (56 percent) still lived in other arrangements; the most common of the other living arrangements was with

mother only (38 percent). Twenty-six percent of the students had five or more siblings; the mean number of siblings was 3.5.

4.   By way of comparison, in a study involving a random sample of minority inner-city males in the ninth and tenth grades in Washington, D.C., Altschuler and Brounstein (1991) found that 10 percent of their subjects had sold drugs. Callahan and Rivara (1992) found that 10 percent of their Seattle eleventh-grade respondents (male and female) had sold drugs.

5.   Overall, our decision to survey incarcerated juveniles and high school students means that we have no data on the large group of urban youth who were neither in school nor incarcerated. Given the substantial high school dropout rates in the cities we surveyed, this is *not* a trivial omission. Still, we could find no practical way to obtain a large or "representative" sample of this group. Fagan et al. (1986) compared school dropouts to students in inner-city schools in the same neighborhoods and both groups to a sample of incarcerated youth. The school dropouts fell between the students and the incarcerated youth in prevalence of every type of delinquency examined in their study.

6.   Survey items utilized in this section included the following: Inmates were asked if "any of your brothers and sisters have ever . . . " "committed a serious crime," "been arrested for a crime," or "served time in a prison or jail?" (response categories: yes, no, don't know). Students were asked only the sibling "serious crime" item. Regarding guns among family members and friends, students were asked: "Does anyone who currently lives in your house or apartment own a handgun of any sort?" (response categories: yes, no) and "Have any of your brothers and sisters ever owned a handgun?" (response categories: yes, no, don't know). Inmates were asked, "Have any of your brothers and sisters ever owned a gun?" (response categories: yes, no, don't know). Both samples were asked whether (a) "the people you hang around with [hung around with, for inmates]" and (b) "males in your family—your father, brothers, uncles, cousins, and so on" (a) owned a gun and (b) "made a habit of carrying guns outside their homes." We have dichotomized responses into yes or no. Regarding victimization, inmates were asked if they had *ever* been, and students if, *in school or on their way to or from school in the last few years*, they had been "threatened or shot at with a gun," "stabbed with a knife," "beaten up," or (students only) "injured by some other weapon [not a gun or knife]." We have dichotomized responses into yes or no.

7.   The annual General Social Survey conducted by the National Opinion Research Center occasionally asks national samples of adult respondents whether they had ever been "threatened with a gun or shot at." The proportion responding yes is always approximately 20 percent.

The experience is surprisingly common in the U.S. population as a whole, but some *four times* more common among the incarcerated youth in our sample.

8.   By way of comparison, analysis of national victimization data (Bastion and Taylor 1991) found, among students of all types (male and female, from urban as well as suburban areas, enrolled in both private and public and troubled and untroubled schools), 25 percent who had been violently attacked, and 4 percent of those who had not feared an attack at school. The same percentages avoided specific places in their schools out of fear of being victimized.

9.   The evident willingness of our respondents to employ violence to redress insult or injury to their families suggests, perhaps, that "family values" remain much stronger among inner-city residents than some social commentators would have us believe.

10.   Several studies of adult felons have suggested that a history of juvenile criminality is the single best predictor of high-rate criminal activity among adults (Chaiken and Chaiken 1982; Visher 1991; Wolfgang, Thornberry, and Figlio 1987; Wright and Rossi 1986:49–50). As these studies have also found, serious, hard-core felons (whether adult or juvenile) tend to begin their criminal activities at a very early age. The majority of our incarcerated juveniles had committed at least one armed crime and had experienced at least one arrest before they were legally old enough to drive.

11.   It is worth emphasizing, as other researchers also have noted (Akers 1992; Fagan et al. 1986), that alcohol and marijuana use was far more common among our respondents than was the use of harder drugs. Nearly 60 percent of the high school students had used alcohol, the majority no more than "a few times" in the last year or so. A quarter had used marijuana, the majority also no more than "a few times" in the last year or so. Similar patterns characterized the incarcerated juveniles: 82 percent had used alcohol at least occasionally in the year or so before their current incarceration, and 84 percent had used marijuana, though most had used each more than "a few times."

3

GUNS IN THE HANDS OF KIDS

> That [.38 caliber revolver] was the third gun I owned.
> It cost me a bag of dope.
>
> —a nineteen-year-old Shreveport, Louisiana, youth
> convicted of murdering a man during a robbery

The media depiction of the firearms environment for juveniles is one in which guns of all types, even sophisticated military-style weapons, are widely and easily available. The average inner-city youth seemingly need only approach a street source, pay but a few dollars, and depart with a firearm. However, no one has documented any of these perceptions systematically, especially regarding the *types* of guns youths are obtaining. How many and what types of guns do inner-city and criminally active youths actually possess? Do they own or borrow their guns? Who supplies the firearms to juveniles? Are the sources always illegal? Are the guns easily obtained? Can they be had cheaply? Is cost not an issue because most guns are stolen by the youth who possess them?

We begin our quest for answers to these questions by assessing the numbers and types of guns owned by youth in our two samples. To measure firearms possession, we gave the respondents a list of firearms and asked them to check which they had owned or possessed (a) over the course of their lifetimes and (b) immediately prior to incarceration (for inmates) or at the time of the survey (for students). Types included (a) hunting and target rifles, (b) military-style automatic or semiautomatic rifles, (c) regular shotguns, (d) sawed-off shotguns, (e) revolvers (also called "regular handguns"), (f) automatic or semiautomatic handguns, (g) derringers or other single-shot handguns, (h) homemade guns (also called "zip guns"). No distinction was made between automatic and semiautomatic weapons because pilot study interviews indicated that juveniles often failed to make such distinctions. Authorities in the area (police, gun experts, criminologists) all suggest, however, that few juveniles possess truly automatic weapons; rather, theirs more likely are semiautomatic.

Numbers and Types of Guns

Inmates and Guns

Table 3.1 presents data on gun possession among the inmate sample; at least regarding this group, the media depiction is largely accurate. Eighty-six percent of the inmates had owned at least one firearm at some time in their young lives;[1] 83 percent owned a gun at the time they were incarcerated.[2] A large majority of the sample (73 percent) had owned three or more *types* of guns in their lifetimes; 54 percent had possessed three or more *types* of guns just prior to being locked up. Nearly two-thirds (65 percent) had owned at least three firearms of any type just before being jailed. In short, these young inmates tended to own guns in both quantity and variety.

Among these youths, the revolver was the most commonly owned firearm; 72 percent had owned a revolver at some time in their lives, and 58 percent owned one at the time of their current incarceration. Next in popularity were automatic and semiautomatic handguns. Two-thirds of the sample had owned such a gun at some time; 55 percent owned one

Table 3.1.   Inmate Gun Possession[a]

Firearm type	Ever owned		Owned just prior to confinement	
	%	(N)	%	(N)
Any type of gun	86	(811)	83	(815)
Target or hunting rifle	38	(804)	22	(823)
Military-style automatic or semiautomatic rifle	46	(808)	35	(823)
Regular shotgun	60	(807)	39	(823)
Sawed-off shotgun	63	(811)	51	(823)
Revolver	72	(809)	58	(823)
Automatic or semiautomatic handgun	66	(816)	55	(823)
Derringer or single-shot handgun	32	(779)	19	(822)
Homemade (Zip) handgun	11	(774)	6	(823)
Owned 3 or more *types* of guns	73	(744)	54	(822)
Owned 3 or more of *any type of gun* just prior to confinement			65	(815)

[a] Measurement described in text.

at the time of their incarceration. The shotgun, whether sawed-off or unaltered, also represented a major weapon of choice. More than half the sample (51 percent) possessed a sawed-off shotgun at the time of their incarceration; 63 percent had owned one at some time. Relevant percentages for regular shotguns were 39 and 60, respectively. (A bit less than half, 47 percent, reported that they personally had cut down a shotgun or rifle to make it easier to carry or conceal at some point in their lives.) Next in popularity were the military-style automatic and semi-automatic rifles that have figured so prominently in recent media accounts. Nearly half our respondents said that they had owned such a weapon at some time; more than a third (35 percent) had owned one at the time they went to prison. Other types of guns—regular hunting rifles, derringers, zip guns, etc.—found little favor, having been owned at the time of incarceration by fewer than a quarter.

Absent additional data, it is hard to be certain which aspects of the pattern of ownership reflect preferences and which aspects reflect availability (see below, "Choosing a Handgun," for further comment on this issue). Considering the ease with which these young felons obtained firearms and the number and variety of guns apparently in circulation in their neighborhoods (also see below), it is a reasonable assumption that they possessed what they preferred to possess and that differential availability had little or no import. There was an evident preference for concealable firearms (handguns and sawed-off shotguns), but hard-to-conceal shoulder weapons, whether military-style or not, were also quite common. These details, however, while of some interest, are as nothing compared to the broad patterns. Four in five incarcerated juveniles in our sample owned at least one gun when they were incarcerated; two-thirds owned three or more guns; one-third owned a military-style rifle.

Students and Guns

Similar patterns of ownership, although on a considerably diminished scale, were found for the high school students as well (Table 3.2). Nearly a third (30 percent) had owned at least one gun in their lives; 22 percent possessed a gun at the time the survey was completed. The most commonly owned weapon was again the revolver (29 percent over the lifetime), followed by the automatic or semiautomatic handgun (27 percent). Fifteen percent owned (or possessed) a revolver, and 18 percent an automatic or semiautomatic handgun at the time of the study.[3] Fifteen percent owned three or more guns when they were surveyed. Shoulder weapons of all sorts were less likely to be owned by the students than were handguns; still, 14 percent had owned a sawed-off

Table 3.2.   Student Gun Possession[a]

Firearm type	Ever owned		Currently owned	
	%	(N)	%	(N)
Any type of gun	30	(733)	22	(741)
Target or hunting rifle	13	(731)	8	(728)
Military-style automatic or semiautomatic rifle	14	(729)	6	(728)
Regular shotgun	14	(730)	10	(728)
Sawed-off shotgun	14	(728)	9	(728)
Revolver	29	(734)	15	(728)
Automatic or semiautomatic handgun	27	(732)	18	(728)
Derringer or single-shot handgun	9	(728)	4	(728)
Homemade (Zip) handgun	11	(725)	4	(727)
Owned 3 or more types of guns	13	(718)	6	(727)
Currently owns 3 or more guns of any type			15	(741)

[a] Measurement described in text.

shotgun at some time, 14 percent had owned an unmodified shotgun, and 14 percent had owned a military-style rifle (6 percent owned a military-style rifle at the time of the survey). In the general gun-owning population, shoulder weapons are about twice as numerous as handguns (Kleck 1991:47), so it is perhaps noteworthy that the students in this sample were more likely to own handguns than shoulder weapons.

Owning versus Carrying Guns

The questions addressed so far have involved guns that our respondents had owned (or considered "theirs" even if they did not own them). Obviously, one need not actually own a gun in order to carry one. Since most of the incarcerated juveniles in our sample (83 percent) owned a gun of their own at the time of their arrest, the distinction may be relatively meaningless for them. But it is easy to imagine high school students who carry guns that they do not own (for example, guns that have been borrowed from or otherwise made available by friends and family members, or possibly guns that are jointly owned by multiple

Table 3.3. Frequency (%) of Gun Carrying—Inmates
and Students[a]

Inmates	
In two years preceding confinement, carried gun outside home, including in car (N = 802):	
All the time	24
Most of the time	31
Only now and then	29
Never	16
Students	
Currently carry gun outside home, including car, but not including in school (N = 699):	
All the time	4
Most of the time	8
Only now and then	23
Never	65
Currently carrying gun in school (N = 709)	
All the time	1.5
Most of the time	1.5
Only now and then	6
Never	91

[a] Measurement described in text.

students). It is possible, in other words, that our focus on ownership in fact produces an *under*estimation of the number of guns in the hands of the students in our study.

Table 3.3 reports findings on gun-carrying behavior.[4] Among the inmate sample, carrying a firearm was about as common as owning one: 55 percent *carried* a gun "all of the time" or "most of the time" in the year or two before being incarcerated, and 84 percent *carried* a gun at least "only now and then," the latter figure nearly identical to the percentage who owned a gun. Among the student sample, carrying a gun at least occasionally was *more common* than gun ownership. Twenty-two percent of the students owned a gun at the time of the survey; 12 percent of them reported currently *carrying* a gun "all of the time" or "most of the time," and another 23 percent did so at least "only now and then," for a combined percentage of 35 *percent who carried firearms regularly or occasionally.* Thus, by this more liberal measure, guns were in the hands of one out of three male, central-city high school students we surveyed. Beyond this, 3 percent of the students reported carrying a gun to school "all of the time" or "most of the time;" an additional 6 percent did so "only now and then."

[handwritten annotation: hand gun most common among inmates & students prefer auto system, or revolvers.]

Handguns w _____ type of gun among both inmates and stu _____ to be sure, were likely to have owned a number and variety of different guns; the students less so, but both groups owned more handguns than shoulder weapons. What, then, did these youths look for in choosing a handgun? What were the characteristics of the handguns they actually owned?

We asked inmates (but not students) to imagine that they had just been released from prison and had decided to obtain a handgun. Would they prefer a revolver or an automatic or semiautomatic handgun? The respondents expressed a strong preference for automatic and semi-automatic handguns over revolvers; 64 percent would prefer the former, 9 percent the latter (the remainder said it would make no difference to them). We find this surprising since, among the guns actually owned at the point of arrest, revolvers were slightly more numerous than auto-matics and semiautomatics. However, 55 percent of the inmates in fact did own an automatic or semiautomatic handgun when incarcerated, which implies that most who *preferred* such guns owned them, with many owning revolvers as well. Whatever the ownership patterns or the reasons behind them, automatic and semiautomatic handguns were the sidearms of preference among our respondents.

Table 3.4. Features of Respondent's Most Recent Handgun
(for Respondents Who Had Ever Owned a Handgun)[a]

Feature	Inmates		Students	
	%	(N)	%	(N)
Handgun type		(647)		(228)
Automatic	29		24	
Semiautomatic	28		25	
Revolver	36		42	
Other (single-shot, etc.)	7		9	
Caliber		(593)		(224)
.22	13		16	
.25	8		13	
.32	4		5	
.357	13		10	
.38	16		16	
.44	4		3	
.45	9		11	
9 millimeter	33		26	

[a] Measurement described in text.

Table 3.5. "Very Important" Handgun Features[a]

[handwritten annotation: All prefer bigger caliber weapons. Look for fire power equally construction & difficulty in tracing]

Feature		(N)	...nts	(N)
Cheap	26	(703)	27	(589)
Easily concealed	43	(705)	36	(577)
Accurate	56	(694)	52	(580)
Easy to shoot	58	(716)	53	(582)
Scary looking	21	(690)	15	(583)
Good-looking	35	(697)	24	(584)
Lot of firepower	68	(704)	48	(584)
Well made	66	(707)	56	(587)
Not easily traced	66	(708)	52	(580)
Uses cheap ammo	23	(688)	26	(577)
Ammo easily obtained	46	(693)	43	(578)
Better than police use	36	(703)	26	(580)

[a] Measurement described in text.

Students and inmates who reported ever owning a handgun were asked to describe the characteristics of the *most recent* handgun they had owned (Table 3.4). (If a respondent owned more than one handgun at the time of the survey, he was asked to describe the one he had *obtained* most recently.) Among these most recently acquired handguns, the automatics and semiautomatics predominated: 57 percent of the inmates' and 49 percent of the students' most recent handguns were automatics or semiautomatics. The percentages owning revolvers as their most recent handgun (among those who owned any handgun) were 36 and 42 for inmates and students, respectively, with small proportions (7 and 9 percent) owning other types of handguns. Regardless of type, both inmates and students tended to own large-caliber guns. Three-fourths of the inmates and two-thirds of the students who owned handguns possessed guns of large caliber,[5] with the 9 mm showing up as the most popular caliber of all. In short, cheap, small caliber weapons (often called Saturday Night Specials) were of little interest to our respondents.

The preferences inferred from patterns of ownership are confirmed in direct questions about desirable handgun features. We asked respondents (both samples) what features, if they were looking for a handgun, they considered important; Table 3.5 displays the percentages of those who rated various features as "very important" (as opposed to "somewhat important" and "not important"). The profile of desirable features was remarkably similar in both groups. Among inmates, the three highest rated traits were firepower, quality of construction, and difficulty in

get guns from
family, friends + theft
"drug dealers" and addicts

tracing ownership, ～～ by being easy to shoot and accurate. Among students, quality of construction was the highest rated trait, followed by being easy to shoot, accurate, untraceable, and with high firepower. Neither inmates nor students indicated much preference for small, cheap guns, nor were they attracted to ephemeral characteristics of weapons such as "scary looking" or "good looking." The preference clearly was for high-firepower hand weapons that were well-made, accurate, easy to shoot and not easily traced.

Sample was limited

Where and How Juveniles Obtain Guns

Our findings to this point indicate that most types of guns are relatively abundant and readily accessible to juveniles—at least to those in our limited samples. Regarding access, we asked our respondents how difficult they thought it would be to obtain a gun if they desired one ("upon release" for the incarcerated youth). Seventy percent of the inmates and 41 percent of the students felt that they could get a gun with "no trouble at all"; an additional 17 percent of the inmates and 24 percent of the students said it would be "only a little trouble."[6] Only 13 percent of the inmates and 35 percent of the students perceived access to guns as a "lot of trouble" or "nearly impossible." Whether these perceptions were entirely accurate is a different matter, of course, but they are certainly consistent with the ownership data already reviewed.

After the question about ease of access, we asked both groups of respondents to indicate the ways they would go about getting the gun. Responses are shown in Table 3.6. Note that multiple responses were allowed and frequent, which is to say that most respondents felt there were numerous ways that they might obtain a firearm.

It is entirely obvious from these data that family, friends, and street sources were the main sources of guns for the juveniles in our samples. Drug dealers and addicts seemed to be the major suppliers after family, friends, and other street sources, this for both inmates and students. Purchasing a gun at a gun shop (or asking someone else to do so—see below) was perceived by 28 percent of the students as a reliable method; only 12 percent of the inmates considered it so (or viewed it as necessary). Theft was twice as likely to be mentioned by the inmates as by the students, although relative to other sources, it was not prominent for either group.

In addition to asking our respondents how they would go about obtaining a gun if they decided they needed one, we asked a number of questions about where and how they had in fact obtained their most

Table 3.6. Likely Means of Obtaining Guns[a]

Source	Inmates (%) (N = 738)	Students (%) (N = 623)
Already have one	46	26
Steal from a person or car	14	7
Steal from house or apartment	17	8
Steal from a store or pawnshop	8	4
Borrow one from family member or friend	45	53
Buy one from family member or friend	36	35
Get one off the street	54	37
Get one from a drug dealer	36	22
Get one from a junkie	35	22
Buy one from gun shop	12	28

[a] Item: "How would you go about getting a gun if you decided you wanted one?" (multiple responses permitted).

recent handguns, military-style weapons, and conventional rifles and shotguns, respectively. The patterns of actual acquisition closely mirrored the results reported in Table 3.6 (these data are not shown in the tables). Informal purchases, swaps, and trades with family, friends, acquaintances, and street sources were the predominant means of gun acquisition for both inmates and high school students; conventional cash transactions with legitimate over-the-counter retailers were uncommon (although somewhat more common for students than inmates).

These findings suggest, perhaps, that there is little need to seek guns through theft (or to bother with normal retail outlets) when they are readily available through personal contacts (friends and family members) or easily obtained through street sources. It is worth noting in this connection that while relatively few inmates mentioned theft as a means through which they would attempt to obtain a gun upon release, far more had actually stolen guns at some time in their lives. About 30 percent of the inmates said they had stolen rifles, shotguns, and military-style weapons; 50 percent had stolen revolvers; and 44 percent had stolen automatic or semiautomatic handguns at some point in their criminal careers.

We also asked the locations from which they had stolen guns. Usually, it was from houses and apartments (42 percent) or cars (35 percent). When the inmates sold or traded their guns, they did so to friends (31 percent had done so) or other trusted persons (23 percent had sold or traded a gun to a fellow gang member, for instance). Thus, these juvenile inmates both supplied guns to and obtained guns from the informal network of family, friends, and street sources.

Guns are easily stolen and they are apparently stolen in large numbers by both juvenile and adult criminals, not so much because felons look for guns to steal but because guns are commonly owned consumer goods that are encountered routinely during crimes (Wright and Rossi 1986:Ch. 10). Since our respondents could only trace the lineage of their firearms to the persons from whom they obtained them, our data are inadequate to estimate the percentage of the juvenile firearms supply that originally enters the chain of commerce through theft, but the percentage must certainly be a large one. Guns obtained from addicts, drug dealers, and other street sources are almost certainly stolen weapons in the large majority; otherwise, the street price of guns (see below) presumably would be much higher. And obviously, many of the guns that our respondents obtained from their interpersonal networks were stolen somewhere along the way. It is therefore highly likely that theft and burglary were the ultimate source of many (perhaps most) of the guns possessed by the juveniles in our study, but only occasionally the proximate source; firearms in circulation (through theft or other means) were sufficiently numerous that a youth seeking a gun need only have checked his network of family, friends, and street contacts to obtain one. Besides, shopping around in the network could better produce the type of weapon the juvenile desired; burglary and theft left the type to fate.

The role of the personal network in obtaining guns is demonstrated by yet another finding. Federal law bars juveniles from purchasing firearms through normal retail outlets; the age cutoff is eighteen for rifles and shotguns and twenty-one for handguns. This provision of the law is readily circumvented by persuading someone who is of legal age to make the purchase in one's behalf, and so we asked both groups of respondents whether they had ever done so. Thirty-two percent of the inmates and 18 percent of the student respondents had indeed asked someone to purchase a gun for them in a gun shop, pawnshop, or other retail outlet. When queried of whom they had asked to purchase these guns, 49 percent of the inmates and 52 percent of the students mentioned a friend; 14 percent of the inmates and 18 percent of the students had turned to family members. Only 7 and 6 percent of the inmates and students, respectively, had sought help from strangers. Returning to Table 3.6, we recall that, for inmates, purchase from a gun shop was viewed as a far less likely means of quick acquisition of a gun than procuring one from an informal source. However, a large percentage actually had used the gun shop indirectly as a source at least once, by asking someone else to make a purchase for them. It seems then that the inmates had access to an informal network that made gun acquisition cheaper and easier; turning to retail channels was generally not necessary. Less streetwise and less hardened, perhaps, the students saw

Table 3.7. Cost of Most Recent Firearm (for Respondents Who Had Purchased Gun for Cash)[a]

Gun Type	Inmates (%)			Students (%)		
	Total	Retail	Informal	Total	Retail	Informal
Handguns						
Less than $50	41	17	21	21	0	25
$50–$100	24	22	48	53	27	58
More than $100	35	61	31	26	73	17
N	235	23	201	64	11	48
Military-style rifles						
Less than $100	22	28	21	28	0	29
$100–$300	48	7	50	21	40	45
More than $300	30	65	29	51	60	35
N	165	14	151	38	5	31
Rifles or shotguns						
Less than $100	54	32	51	47	25	52
$100–$150	13	14	20	29	25	28
More than $150	33	54	29	24	50	20
N	153	19	134	30	4	25

[a] By way of interpretation of the results, of 235 inmates whose most recently acquired gun was a handgun and who said they paid cash for that handgun, 41% paid $50 or less and 35% paid $100 or more; likewise, among 38 students whose most recently acquired gun was a military rifle that had been purchased for cash, 51% paid more than $300 for it. "Retail" means a gun shop, pawnshop, or other retail outlet; "informal" is a cash purchase from any other source.

themselves as more dependent upon the retail shop if they needed a gun, although only 18 percent had ever used that source.[7]

Aside from convenience, there is another good reason why juveniles might prefer informal and street sources over normal retail outlets. Guns obtained from informal and street sources are considerably less expensive. We asked our respondents (both groups) how much they had paid for their most recent handgun, military-style rifle, and standard rifle or shotgun, respectively. (The question was only asked of respondents who indicated that the acquisition had been a cash purchase, as opposed to barter, trade, or theft). The findings (Table 3.7) suggest that street prices were quite low. The substantial majority of handguns and conventional shoulder weapons obtained by our respondents in a cash transaction with an informal source were purchased for one hundred dollars or less; most of the military-style rifles obtained from such sources were purchased for three hundred dollars or less. Considering the general quality of the firearms in question (see above), the cash prices paid on the street were clearly much less than the normal retail cost.

The sources and methods by which the juveniles in our samples obtained guns are strikingly similar to the sources and methods exploited by adult felons for the same purpose (Wright and Rossi 1986); in both cases, informal, off-the-record transactions predominate (as they very well may even among adult, nonfelon buyers). Most of the sources for both juvenile and adult felon firearms can be counted on to ask no questions; most of the transactions are entirely private affairs that are (for all practical purposes) impossible to regulate and leave no discernible trace. Keeping guns out of the hands of juveniles then apparently involves exactly the same difficulties as keeping them out of the hands of adult felons. While many mechanisms have been suggested to accomplish this worthwhile goal, none has yet proven very effective (Kleck 1991:Ch. 10).

Dealing Guns

Given the means and sources of firearms acquisition for both inmate and student respondents, it is obvious that there is a large, informal street market in guns, one in which persons like our inmate respondents are likely to be regular suppliers as well as frequent consumers. Table 3.8

Table 3.8. Gun Sales by Inmates

Item	%	N
Percentage who have dealt guns[a]	51	732
If respondent ever dealt guns, what was the source of guns?		371[b]
Theft from cars and houses	37	
Theft from stores or shipping trucks	8	
Got them from drug addicts	26	
Got them from drug dealers	6	
Bought them in state	7	
Bought them out of state	16	
Has respondent gone to places with easy gun laws to buy guns for later sale?[c]		759
A few times	15	
Many times	5	

[a] Respondents who had "personally been involved in dealing guns," that is, buying, selling, or trading for a lot of guns.
[b] N represents those who had dealt guns.
[c] Measurement described in text.

reports findings on gun-dealing among the inmate sample (these questions were not asked of students). Fifty-one percent reported having dealt guns (personally bought, sold, or traded a *lot* of guns). Of those who described themselves as dealers, the majority reported their most common source as theft from homes or cars and acquisitions from drug addicts. Sixteen percent had bought guns for purposes of gun dealing out of state; another 7 percent had done so in state; nearly one in ten (8 percent) had stolen guns in quantity from stores or off trucks during shipment.

The findings reported in Table 3.8 suggest that there were two very different types of "gun dealers" in our inmate sample. One was comprised of juveniles who occasionally came into possession of surplus firearms and then sold or traded them to street sources. They may have come across firearms in the course of burglaries or break-ins, or taken firearms from drug addicts in exchange for drugs, but they were not systematically in the business of gun-dealing; their involvement in gun deals was mainly a matter of disposing of surplus merchandise for which they had no other use. The other group was more systematic in its gun-dealing activities and looked on gun deals as a business, seeking, if necessary, to purchase guns both in and out of state to supply their consumers. This group presumably would include the one inmate in five (see Table 3.8) who had gone (a few times or many times) to states "with very easy gun laws" to buy up guns for resale in their own neighborhoods, in direct defiance of federal firearms laws.[8]

Multivariate Considerations

We noted in the introductory chapter that site was related, apparently not systematically, to some findings of this study. As well, we pointed to general self-report findings that race of the respondent may play a role in his answers to items concerning illegal behavior. To address this issue more directly, we have controlled age and race/ethnicity of the respondent as well as state in which the survey was administered for both samples.[9] For the inmate sample, we have controlled for size of respondent's hometown ("city size") as well. Tables 3.9 (inmates) and 3.10 (students) report the findings of logistic regression analyses concerning the influence of these variables upon whether or not respondents owned automatic or semiautomatic handguns, revolvers, and sawed-off shotguns and whether or not they carried guns routinely ("most of the time" or "all of the time") outside their homes.[10] The analyses are based on samples with missing cases excluded. In the present and in most instances reported in coming chapters, exclusion of missing cases had

Table 3.9. Logistic Regression of Firearm-Related Activities on Sociodemographic and Site Variables—Inmate Sample (N = 803); Beta Coefficients

Variable	Owned Handgun		Owned sawed-off shotgun	Carried gun routinely
	Auto/semi-auto	Revolver		
Age	.098	.022	.041	.056
Race/ethnicity[a]				
Black	−.173	.044	−.095	−.012
Hispanic	−.603*	−.150	−.114	−.337
White	−.506	−.268	−.497	−.598*
City size	.028	.040	−.006	.066
Site[b]				
California	.231	.736*	.891*	.680*
Illinois	−.274	.339	.219	.434
Louisiana	.365	.481	.098	.330
Constant	−1.403	−.679	−.786	−1.285
Model χ^2 (df = 8)	16.060*	16.133*	8.551	23.447*

* $p < .05$.   [a] "Other" omitted.   [b] New Jersey omitted.

little effect on outcome; where a difference was observed (see especially Chapter 6), the results from analyses with missing cases included (via mean substitution) are also reported in footnotes.

For both samples, age had little effect on the behaviors in question; for the inmate sample, size of hometown was similarly without import. Race/ethnicity also had little effect with a few notable exceptions.

Table 3.10. Logistic Regression of Firearm-Related Activities on Sociodemographic and Site Variables—Student Sample (N = 723); Beta Coefficients

Variable	Owned Handgun		Owned sawed-off shotgun	Carried gun routinely
	Auto/semi-auto	Revolver		
Age	.105	−.017	.095	.098
Race/Ethnicity[a]				
Black	1.276*	.485	.354	.448
Hispanic	.074	−.093	−.601	−.117
Site[b]				
California	.961*	.803*	2.810*	1.576*
Illinois	.888*	.948*	2.919*	1.352*
Louisiana	.620	.338	2.450*	1.221*
Constant	−4.986*	−2.427	−6.647*	−5.128*
Model χ^2 (df = 6)	27.035*	12.211	23.261*	13.920*

* $p < .05$.   [a] "Other" omitted.   [b] New Jersey omitted.

Among inmates, Hispanics were less likely than were other inmates to own an automatic or semiautomatic handgun; whites were less likely than were other inmates to carry a gun routinely.[11] Among students, blacks were more likely to own an automatic or semiautomatic handgun. Finally, among inmate respondents, Californians consistently were more involved in most of the behaviors in question. Among students, considerable site influence was obvious regarding these same behaviors. It seems wise, therefore, to introduce controls for all of these variables in multivariate analyses presented in later chapters.

Summary

Owning and carrying guns were fairly common behaviors among our respondents, especially among the inmates we surveyed. The guns they possessed and carried were high-quality, sophisticated weapons, the most common of which were revolvers. The possession of military-style assault weapons was common but less so than media attention to that type of weapon would suggest. Despite their apparent quality, these firearms were acquired cheaply and most often through friends and family members and secondarily from street sources. When respondents stole guns, their common targets were homes and cars. When they sold or traded guns, they generally did so within the same network from which they obtained them—family members, friends, and street sources. Gun dealing had been practiced by half of the inmate respondents prior to their incarceration. Most such activity was of a lesser scale: the unsystematic sale or exchange of arms obtained through burglaries or drug deals.

Possession of and commerce in firearms by juveniles are problematic, but this problem is relatively minor compared to the more pressing issue of the actual use of guns by respondents in our study. Are the firearms owned by juveniles of the type we surveyed used for crime? Are they status symbols? Is a gun the perceived means of survival in the inner city? These questions form the heart of Chapter 4.

Notes

1.   Of those who had ever owned a gun, it is notable that 67 percent acquired their first firearm by the age of fourteen.

2.   By way of comparison, Callahan et al. (1993) report that 59 percent of their sample of youths held in a Seattle-area short-term detention facility reported owning a handgun.

3.   By way of comparison, in their survey of eleven-grade Seattle students (from all types of schools), Callahan and Rivara (1992) found that 11 percent of the male respondents had owned a handgun.

4.   Specifically, inmates were asked, "Thinking about the year or two before you came to this facility, about how often would you say you carried a gun with you when you were outside your home (including in your car)?" Students were asked, "About how often would you say you carry a gun with you when you are outside your home but not at school (that is, when you are not on school property)—including in your car?" As well, students were asked about how often they carried guns when at school. For each item, possible responses were "all of the time," "most of the time," "only now and then," and "never."

5.   For purposes of this report, "large"- or "big"-caliber firearms are those whose calibers were reported as .357, .38, .44, .45, or 9 millimeter. "Small"-caliber guns are those of .22, .25, and .32 caliber.

6.   Callahan and Rivara (1992) report that 47 percent of their eleventh-grade, male respondents in Seattle viewed access to a handgun as nonproblematic.

7.   Our data were gathered, of course, prior to the enactment of the Brady Law, which imposes a mandatory five-day waiting period for purchase of handguns, ostensibly so that local police can conduct a background check on potential purchasers. Having someone who is "clean" (e.g., old enough, no prior felony convictions, not otherwise proscribed from buying firearms) make proxy purchases in one's behalf is one among many obvious methods by which to circumvent Brady and related measures imposed at the point of retail sale—a method that evidently occurred to about one in three of our inmate respondents and one in five of our student respondents. We can only wonder what these percentages would look like presently, a year after Brady's passage.

8.   Respondents were asked: "Some of the people we have talked to have told us that they have gone to places with very easy gun laws, bought up a lot of guns, and brought them back to their own neighborhoods to deal. Have you personally ever done something like that?" Response categories included "never," "just once," "a few times," "many times."

9.   As nominal variables, race/ethnicity and site were entered into the regression equations as dummy variables. For the inmate sample, respondents who were not white, black, or Hispanic were treated as the category against which to compare others. For students, white and others were combined into one reference group against which to compare blacks and Hispanics. New Jersey was designated the "omitted" or reference category among the four states serving as research sites.

10.   We also categorized gun-carrying as "none" and "any" ("only

now and then," "most of the time," "all of the time"). In this, and analyses reported in coming chapters, differences in findings as a function of measurement of gun-carrying are reported in footnotes.

11.　When analyses are conducted with missing cases included via mean substitution, Hispanic respondents are no more likely than others to own automatic or semiautomatic weapons. Nor are whites more likely to carry firearms routinely. In both cases, the relationship barely misses statistical significance at the .05 level.

4

GUN POSSESSION:
CRIME, STATUS, OR PROTECTION

I got it [a handgun] just in case something happens. Every time somebody gets shot, everybody says, "Yo, man, I'm getting me a gun." I ain't letting anybody smoke me.

—Kevin, from Jersey City, New Jersey, on why he bought his first gun at age seventeen (quoted in a Newhouse News Service article appearing in the *New Orleans Times-Picayune*)

Conventional wisdom suggests that guns in the hands of kids equate to crime by kids. Without indicting the logic of this position, it is also fair to say that it reflects the worries of real and potential victims more than their thoughtful analysis of all the roles guns may play in the lives of youth. For example, 2 percent of the students in one national-level study had carried a weapon (including, but not limited to guns) to school for *protection* at least once during a six-month period (Bastion and Taylor 1991; see also Asmussen 1992). In a second national-level study, one in five high school students reported carrying a weapon (including, but not limited to guns; also not limited to weapon-carrying in schools) during the past thirty days for *protection* or *use in a fight* (U.S. Department of Health and Human Services 1991).

Thus, the issue of motivation for possession and carrying of firearms remains open for the present. To what ends are guns carried by youth: self-protection, intimidation, crime, status enhancement? Without examining the importance of guns as seen through their eyes, we cannot begin to understand, let alone direct policy toward this problem. In this chapter, we attempt to do precisely that: to examine why youth carry and use firearms through analysis of a number of survey responses pertinent to the issue.

Guns and Crime

We noted previously that more than half of our inmate respondents made a habit of carrying guns nearly all the time and that almost all carried guns at least occasionally. Even among the high school student respondents, one in three had carried a gun at least "only now and then." We also found, as expected in a group of wards in maximum security reformatories, that the criminal records of the inmates in our study were extensive. Half had committed armed robberies, for example. Far less criminal on average, the student respondents nonetheless lived in environments in which crime was common: two-thirds had had encounters with the police; one-quarter had committed nontrivial property crimes.

To gain an enhanced sense of the seriousness of the criminality of our inmate respondents, we asked them several questions specifically about crimes committed with guns and other weapons (see Table 4.1).[1] Seventy-three percent had used a weapon of some sort to commit a crime at least once. About 80 percent of those who had ever committed a crime while so armed did so before they were sixteen years of age. Forty-four percent reported using a weapon to commit a crime at least weekly. Nearly two of every three respondents (63 percent) had used a gun to commit a crime. Better than two-thirds of the incarcerated juveniles who had committed gun-related crimes did so before age sixteen. Forty percent of the inmates had procured a gun specifically for use in a crime. Seventy-six percent claimed to have fired a gun at someone at some time. Fifty-nine percent had committed a crime with a revolver, and 56 percent had done so with an automatic or semiautomatic firearm. Fifty-five percent reported actually firing a gun during the commission of a crime.[2] Nine percent of the student sample, by contrast, reported using a weapon (not necessarily a gun) to commit a crime (finding not reported in Table 4.1).[3] In short, the popular fear concerning victimization by armed juveniles is not wholly unfounded.

Our immediate task is to gain some sense of patterns of gun use by respondents who reported having committed violent acts. We take care here to assume no particular causal direction regarding the guns-crime relationship. It may well be, for example, that predators seek out guns or certain types of guns; it may as easily be that persons with guns or certain types of guns are more likely to rob or kill. The former possibility is, of course, a relative truism given that the crimes examined in this study are directly firearm related. As expected, inmate and student respondents involved in violence were indeed significantly more likely than those who were not to own every kind of gun of interest here[4] and to carry firearms routinely, though it is noteworthy that reasonably high percentages of those who did not engage in crimes of violence owned and carried firearms. Involvement in crime was particularly associated with possession of handguns and sawed-off shotguns, less so with possession of regular shotguns and automatic and semiautomatic rifles.

While these findings may not surprise, those displayed in Tables 4.2 and 4.3 may—at least in terms of the *strength* of the associations found

Table 4.1. Committing Crimes with Guns and Other Weapons: Inmates

Item[a]	%
Ever used a *weapon* to commit a crime (N = 806)	
Yes	73
No	27
Age at first weapon use in crime (subsample = 588)	
12 years or under	26
13–15	54
16+	20
Frequency of weapon use in crime (subsample = 588)	
Less than monthly	34
Monthly	22
Weekly	21
Daily	23
Ever used a *gun* for crime? (N = 800)	
Yes	63
No	37
Age at first *gun* use in crime (subsample = 504)	
12 years and under	19
13–15	52
16+	29
Ever procured a gun for crimes (N = 762)	
Yes	40
No	60
Ever shot at someone (N = 801)	
Yes	76
No	24
Ever committed a crime with a revolver (N = 756)	
Yes	59
No	41
Ever committed a crime with an automatic or semiautomatic weapon (N = 758)	
Yes	56
No	44
Ever fired a gun during a crime (N = 800)	
Yes	55
No	45

[a] Measurement described in text.

between types of guns owned and involvement in violent crime. Ownership of any given type of firearm, ownership of three or more guns, and the routine carrying of a gun are all significantly and strongly related to the inmates' violent criminal activity (Table 4.2). Indeed, our ability to predict violence on the basis of gun ownership equals or exceeds our ability to predict gun ownership on the basis of involvement in violence.

Again, however, we note the substantial percentage of non–gun owners who did not engage in the forms of violence examined here.

The findings regarding the inmates are essentially replicated in the student sample. Here we have only one measure of violence: use of a weapon to commit a crime (see above). But we are also able to distinguish students who have been arrested from those who have not and students who have stolen something worth fifty dollars or more from those who have not, and thus to treat these activities as indicators of more general criminality.[5] As the findings in Table 4.3 indicate, in all instances, possession and carrying of a firearm by a student correlate with involvement in violent and property crime and arrest.

For both samples then, it is as likely that gun possession leads to violent crime as it is that violent crime promotes gun possession. More

Table 4.2. Inmates' Involvement in Violent Activity by Gun Ownership and Gun Carrying[a]

Owned/carried firearm	Armed robbery	Procured gun for crime	Fired gun during crime	Fired gun at someone
Revolver				
Yes/no (%)	57/37	48/26	65/40	89/57
(N)	(802)	(754)	(698)	(789)
Auto/semiauto handgun				
Yes/no (%)	59/36	49/27	68/38	90/58
(N)	(802)	(754)	(698)	(789)
Auto/semiauto rifle				
Yes/no (%)	56/44	56/30	43/25	93/67
(N)	(802)	(754)	(698)	(789)
Regular shotgun				
Yes/no (%)	58/42	53/24	71/36	93/58
(N)	(802)	(754)	(698)	(789)
Sawed-off shotgun				
Yes/no (%)	61/35	53/24	71/36	93/58
(N)	(802)	(754)	(698)	(789)
Owned 3 or more guns				
Yes/no (%)	59/30	55/21	74/31	94/53
(N)	(793)	(750)	(691)	(780)
Carried guns routinely[b]				
Yes/no (%)	61/35	55/21	74/31	94/53
(N)	(780)	(777)	(685)	(745)

[a] Measurement described in text. All relationships described in this table are statistically significant. Interpretation: Table displays the percentage of criminals among those who owned or carried guns vs. the percentage of criminals among those who did not. For example, 57% of those who owned a revolver had committed an armed robbery while only 37% of those who did not own a revolver had committed an armed robbery.

[b] Carried gun "most" or "all" of the time preceding confinement.

Table 4.3. Students' Involvement in Criminal Activity by Gun Ownership and Gun Carrying[a]

Owned/carried firearm	Used weapon for crime	Theft of $50+	Arrested
Revolver			
Yes/no (%)	27/7	48/20	66/39
(N)	(668)	(665)	(659)
Auto/semiauto handgun			
Yes/no (%)	20/7	47/19	66/39
(N)	(668)	(665)	(659)
Auto/semiauto rifle			
Yes/no (%)	30/8	47/22	59/41
(N)	(668)	(665)	(659)
Regular shotgun			
Yes/no (%)	32/7	53/21	71/40
(N)	(668)	(665)	(659)
Sawed-off shotgun			
Yes/no (%)	40/7	59/21	67/40
(N)	(668)	(665)	(659)
Owned 2 or more guns			
Yes/no (%)	22/6	46/18	63/38
(N)	(679)	(678)	(672)
Carried guns routinely[b]			
Yes/no (%)	34/7	49/20	66/40
(N)	(651)	(642)	(636)

[a] Measurement described in text. All relationships described in this table are statistically significant. Interpretation: Table displays the precentage of criminals among those who owned or carried guns vs. the percentage of criminals among those who did not. For example, 27% of those who owned a revolver had used a weapon for a crime while only 7% of those who did not own a revolver had used a weapon for a crime.
[b] Carried gun "most" or "all" of the time.

likely still, the findings point less to a *causal* possibility than to an environment characterized by both firearms and crime. Firearms are carried for numerous reasons; they are also useful in the commission of crimes, most of which would be attempted even if firearms were not available. This is suggested particularly by the findings in the last column of Table 4.2: possession and carrying of guns are more strongly linked to an inmate's generally having fired at someone than to having engaged in the predatory offenses indexed in the table (first three columns).

Why do juveniles carry or use firearms in the commission of crimes? Some research attention has been given to possession of guns by criminals as "tools of the trade." Cook (1976) argues, for example, that robbers prefer guns because they permit robbery of more lucrative targets; others point to guns as highly intimidating and thus more facilitative of robbery. Injury to victims is inversely related to the use of a gun as the robber's weapon (Cook 1980; Skogan 1978). Wright and Rossi (1986) argue that much gun use in predatory crimes is motivated by the felon's perceived need to protect himself from potentially aggressive victims. Much regarding choice and use of weapons by criminals likely depends upon whether or not the offenders are "professionals" or "career" offenders (Conklin 1972; Greenwood 1980). Criminologists long have recognized, for example, that injury to robbery victims is often a matter of an amateurish response to a recalcitrant victim by an unprofessional robber (likely to be the more juvenile offender who lacks the skills to gain compliance).

We are able to gain some insight into the issue of the motivations for firearm use in crimes by juveniles through examination of a number of survey items. Specifically, we asked respondents who reported "always" or "usually" being armed with a gun during the commission of a crime the importance of each of five possible reasons for carrying a gun.[6]

Table 4.4 presents the percentage of armed-crime inmates who considered a given reason to carry a weapon during a crime "very important." Two items touched on the intimidating effect of a weapon used in a crime: 45 percent felt a weapon decreased the odds that a victim would resist the offender, and 42 percent reasoned that people do not "mess with" someone with a weapon. However, important though it seems to be for the type of juvenile studied here, intimidation takes a back seat to protection in weapon-related crimes. The two reasons considered most important by the inmates in question pointed to the offender's sense of risk of harm associated with the crime. Eighty percent considered it very important to be ready to defend oneself in a crime, and 58 percent expressed concern that a victim may be armed. In a related vein, 49 percent thought a weapon might facilitate an escape from a crime scene.[7]

The perception of risk to the offender in a crime situation probably is not groundless. A juvenile in the process of deciding to commit a crime contemplates a range of risks and benefits. The benefits consist of financial or other gains. The costs include the possibility of being caught and

Table 4.4. "Very Important" Reasons for Carrying a Weapon During a Crime—Inmates Who Routinely Carried Guns during Crime[a] (N = 393)

Reasons for carrying a gun during crime	Very Important (%)
Have to be ready to defend self	80
Chance victim would be armed	58
Might need weapon to escape	49
Victim won't put up a fight	45
People don't "mess with" armed offender	42

[a] Measurement described in text. Routinely carrying guns refers to the practice of "always" or "usually" arming oneself for crime.

imprisoned as well as being shot (or otherwise injured) in the course of the crime either by the victim, a bystander, or the police. The probability of encountering a victim who possesses a firearm is by no means trivial. Many private citizens claim to own guns for self-defense (Wright et al. 1983). Indeed, 36 percent of the respondents in our study reported having decided at least "a few times" not to commit a crime because they believed the potential victim was armed. Seventy percent of the respondents reported having been "scared off, shot at, wounded, or captured by an armed crime victim."

Gun Dealing, Gun Possession, and Crime

We have to this point concentrated on predatory crime. Our focus on guns necessitates at least a cursory look at a related criminal phenome-

Table 4.5. Inmates' Gun Dealing, Gun Possession, and Criminal Activity[a]

Item[b]	Gun dealing		Sold guns obtained elsewhere	
	(Yes/no)(%)	*(N)*	*(Yes/no)(%)*	*(N)*
Gun possession				
Owned military gun	57/24	(659)	66/39	(738)
Owned shotgun	69/43	(656)	80/54	(734)
Owned sawed-off shotgun	77/41	(659)	85/57	(738)
Owned revolver	82/55	(657)	87/69	(737)
Owned automatic hand-gun	79/46	(664)	80/62	(744)
Carried gun routinely	72/35	(708)	76/47	(732)
Criminal activity				
Burglary	68/53	(662)	78/60	(740)
Robbery	56/33	(659)	66/43	(736)
Homicide	48/20	(611)	63/31	(682)
Property crime for drug money	43/28	(655)	57/33	(733)
Shooting incidents				
Fired gun during crime	88/52	(673)	94/69	(754)
Fired gun at someone	88/54	(656)	96/70	(732)
Willingness to shoot for gain				
OK to shoot someone who has something you want	72/52	(646)	83/59	(723)

[a] All relationships described in this table are statistically significant at least at the .05 level.
[b] All measures utilized in this table have been described earlier in this book.

non: selling guns. We noted in the previous chapter that 51 percent of the inmate respondents reported having dealt guns and that dealers tended to be of two types: juveniles who occasionally came into possession of surplus firearms and then sold or traded them to street sources, and juveniles who were more systematic in their gun-dealing activities and looked on gun deals as a business, seeking (if need be) to purchase guns both in and out of state to supply their consumers.

Those who said they had ever dealt guns, whether systematically or not, were more involved in gun possession, gun use, and criminal activity than those who had not dealt guns at all (Table 4.5, first column); those who were more systematic in their gun deals (having gone out of state to buy guns for resale) were even more involved (Table 4.5, third column). By either measure, inmates who had dealt guns were more likely to own all types of firearms, more likely to carry a gun routinely, more involved in crime and shooting incidents, and more accepting of shooting someone to get something they wanted. In short, for our respondents, dealing firearms seems to have been part of a larger complex of deviant and illegal behavior that also includes owning, carrying and firing guns, committing crimes, and otherwise wreaking social havoc.

Guns as Status Symbols

As aspects of the preceding results suggest, to find that criminal violence and gun ownership, carrying, and dealing are related is not necessarily to find that the reason (or, at least, the primary reason) juveniles own and carry guns is to commit crimes. Indeed, the percentage of inmates who had procured a gun specifically for use in a crime (40 percent) was considerably less than the percentage of inmates who had committed gun-related crimes (63 percent). It is possible then that crimes often were committed with guns that were obtained or carried routinely with other ends in mind.

According to some media reviews of the issue, "respect" is a major element in the decision to carry a gun (Hackett et al. 1988; *New Orleans Times-Picayune* 1993). In this view, the gun is principally a symbolic totem that displays "toughness" or "machismo" and whose primary function is thus to make an impression on one's peers. This portrait does not appear to describe our respondents. Table 4.6 presents findings concerning whether or not the juveniles we surveyed owned and carried guns mainly as a means of achieving or maintaining status among their peers. We asked both inmates and students to agree strongly, agree, disagree, or disagree strongly, "In my crowd, if you don't have a gun people don't

Table 4.6 Guns as a Symbol of Respect among Peers

	Inmates		Students	
Item	*Whole sample*	*Gun carriers*	*Whole sample*	*Gun carriers*
"In my crowd, if you don't have a gun, people don't respect you."				
Strongly disagree (%)	53	50	63	48
Disagree (%)	33	33	27	29
Agree or strongly agree (%)	14	17	10	23
(N)	(745)	(446)	(590)	(85)
"My friends would look down on me if I did not carry a gun."				
Strongly disagree (%)	58	57	67	42
Disagree (%)	31	31	24	33
Agree or strongly agree (%)	11	12	9	25
(N)	(740)	(446)	(579)	(84)

respect you." Eighty-six percent of the inmates and 90 percent of the students *rejected* this statement, most of them strongly. We also asked them to agree or disagree (strongly or otherwise), "My friends would look down on me if I did not carry a gun." Eighty-nine percent of the inmates and 91 percent of the students also *disagreed* with this statement

Table 4.7. When Were Inmates Likely to Carry Guns?[a]

	"Very likely" (%)		
How likely were you to carry a gun when:[a]	*Whole sample* (N = 477)	*Armed robbers*[b] (N = 416)	*Armed criminals*[c] (N = 427)
Doing a drug deal	50	57	71
Raising hell	32	39	43
In a strange area	72	79	86
At night	58	64	74
Hanging out with friends	38	43	49
Friends were carrying guns	39	42	47
Needing protection	75	78	82
Planning to do a crime	37	50	61

[a] Respondents who had carried guns "now and then" or "most of the time". Measurement described in text.
[b] Inmates who had committed armed robbery.
[c] Inmates who "always" or "usually" were armed with a gun when committing a crime.

Table 4.8. "Very Important" Reasons for Purchasing Most Recent Gun[a]

| | Percentage stating that each reason was "very important" | | | | |
| | Inmates | | | Students | |
Gun type	Whole sample	Robbers[b]	Armed criminals[c]	Whole sample	Armed criminals[d]
Military-Style Guns					
(N)	(335)	(224)	(260)	(83)	(33)
Protection	73	74	78	75	78
Enemies had guns	60	60	65	42	79
Use in crimes	40	50	49	e	e
To get someone	43	46	51	25	48
Friends had one	20	23	22	16	33
To impress people	10	12	11	9	12
To sell	11	13	14	6	0
Handguns					
(N)	(611)	(329)	(317)	(180)	(29)
Protection	74	77	82	70	79
Enemies had guns	52	54	61	28	75
Use in crimes	36	47	52	e	e
To get someone	37	44	49	13	33
Friends had one	16	20	20	7	25
To impress people	10	11	10	10	20
To sell	10	13	11	4	0
Rifles or shotguns					
(N)	(470)	(279)	(290)	(107)	(28)
Protection	64	66	73	59	78
Enemies had guns	47	51	56	29	54
Use in crimes	35	48	48	e	e
To get someone	37	43	45	20	37
Friends had one	16	19	21	5	16
To impress people	10	12	11	7	12
To sell	10	11	12	8	4

[a] Measurement described in text.
[b] Inmates who had committed armed robbery.
[c] Inmates who "always" or "usually" were armed with a gun when committing a crime.
[d] Students who had committed a crime with a weapon.
[e] Item not asked of students.

(most, again, strongly). These findings hold as well for inmates and students who had carried guns, though among student gun carriers a somewhat higher percentage of respondents agreed (Table 4.6).

A similar conclusion is evident from the findings presented in Table 4.7. Inmates who said they carried guns at least occasionally but not "all of the time" were asked about the circumstances in which they were most likely to carry a gun.[8] (The question is, of course, meaningless for those who never carried and for those who carried all the time.) The *least* likely circumstance in which inmates would carry guns was when they were "out raising hell," presumably a peer-linked activity. They were also relatively unlikely to carry guns when they were "hanging out with friends" or when they were with friends who were themselves carrying guns. If it were simply a matter of status or reputation, one would expect these to be the *most* (not the least) likely circumstances in which they would carry. These findings pertain not only to the larger sample of inmates but to subsamples of those who had committed armed robbery and those who "always" or "usually" were armed when committing a crime. Finally, we asked both samples about the reasons why they purchased their most recent weapons (Table 4.8).[9] "To impress people" and "because my friends had one" were among the least important of all the reasons we asked about, regardless of weapon type, regardless of involvement in violent predatory crime, and for students and inmates equally. It thus appears that we can dismiss the "symbolism" or "status" hypothesis with a great deal of confidence, at least for the samples studied here.

Guns as Protection

In fact, a number of lines of evidence converge on the possibility—as yet underemphasized in the literature and not well appreciated in the public sector—that the juvenile's decision to arm himself is motivated primarily by a sensed need for self-preservation. Rather than signaling a concern with status, the responses summarized in Tables 4.7 and 4.8 are dominated overwhelmingly by themes of self-protection. Inmates who carried guns did so most frequently when they were in a strange area (72 percent), when they were out at night (58 percent), and whenever they thought they might face a need for self-protection (75 percent). The same themes emerge when we examine responses among subsamples of robbers and armed offenders. Likewise, the results in Table 4.8 indicate that, for any of the three types of guns purchased by either inmates or students, use in crime or to "get someone" was very important for no more than 40 percent. Here too, the desire for protection and the need to arm oneself against enemies were the primary reasons to obtain a gun, easily outpacing all other motivations.

The theme of self-protection is again evident, though less clearly so, in the circumstances in which the inmate respondents had actually *fired* their guns (Table 4.9).[10] Here the most frequent circumstance was "while

Table 4.9. When Had the Inmates Fired Their Guns?

| | Percentage who fired (N) | | |
Circumstance[a]	Whole sample	Robbers[b]	Armed criminals[c]
In self-defense	69 (718)	81 (352)	87 (318)
During a crime	55 (704)	76 (356)	79 (320)
During drug deals	53 (697)	66 (342)	76 (318)
While hanging out with friends	75 (711)	89 (358)	89 (324)
While high or drunk	54 (691)	71 (346)	69 (314)
While fleeing from police	35 (682)	48 (340)	53 (312)
During a fight	61 (709)	75 (351)	80 (321)
To scare someone	66 (720)	80 (359)	76 (325)

[a] Measurement described in text.
[b] Inmates who had committed armed robbery.
[c] Inmates who "always" or "usually" were armed with a gun when committing a crime.

hanging out with friends" (one of the less frequent reasons for carrying a gun; see Table 4.7), regardless of whether or not the respondents had committed violent crimes. The second most frequent circumstance involved self-defense; this also held true regardless of the respondent's involvement in violent crime. Sixty-nine percent of the inmates had fired a gun in what they considered self-defense. More than eight in ten of those who had committed armed robbery or generally were armed when committing crimes had fired in self-defense as well. Aside from the low percentage of inmates who had fired while fleeing from the police, most of the other circumstances examined here drew similar, relatively high percentages across inmate categories: shooting during a crime, firing to scare someone, and firing during drug deals and fights.

The earlier findings regarding reasons for the purchase and carrying of firearms pointed clearly to a perceived need for self-protection among members of both samples. The findings in Table 4.9 suggest a complex of reasons why the inmates (serious offenders who would be expected to have fired guns during crimes) might shoot a gun. That same complex suggests that these juveniles, both by design and by fate, find themselves in circumstances that, in their judgment, require gunfire. It is likely that their distinction between victim and perpetrator is often vague. Most of our inmate respondents had used guns to intimidate others and had had guns used against them. Much of the self-protection they sought, in short, was protection against one another. Likewise, it seems probable that many of our high school student respondents felt some need to protect themselves against one another and nearly certain that they felt a need to protect against the sorts of juveniles represented in the inmate sample.

Multivariate Considerations

In the previous chapter we deemed it wise to control for socio-demographic characteristics and research site when discussing distributions and relationships in this study. In the present chapter, we have found that criminal activity and the perceived need for protection seem to influence the gun-related behaviors of respondents; status enhancement does not seem influential. However, we cannot be sure that these findings hold independently of each other. For this reason, we have entered criminal activity, status enhancement, and need for protection as independent variables in the logistic regression model presented at the conclusion of the last chapter. Additionally, a fourth dependent vari-

Table 4.10. Logistic Regression of Firearm-Related Activities on Motivational, Sociodemographic, and Site Variables—Inmate Sample (*N* = 632)

	Beta coefficients				
	Owned handgun		Owned sawed-off	Carried gun	Fired gun
Variable	auto/semiauto	Revolver	shotgun	routinely	at someone
Criminal activity	.266*	.182*	.265*	.318*	.423*
Status enhancement	.036	−.049	.050	.202	.006
Need for protection	.769*	.538*	.620*	.892*	1.152*
Age	.047	.023	.045	−.010	.039
Race/ethnicity[a]					
Black	.088	.227	.085	.298	.653
Hispanic	−.304	.233	.251	−.100	.307
White	.134	.007	−.285	−.288	−.132
City size	.020	.009	.075	.012	−.011
Site[b]					
California	−.247	.639*	.258	.370	.555
Illinois	−.834*	.432	.105	.283	.599
Louisiana	.475	.737*	.453	.257	.413
Constant	−2.145	−1.865*	−2.311	−2.343	−2.463
Model χ^2 (df = 11)	128.522*	77.818*	103.080*	162.846*	187.486*

* $p < .05$.
[a] "Other" omitted.
[b] New Jersey omitted.

Table 4.11. Logistic Regression of Firearm-Related Activities on Motivational, Sociodemographic, and Site Variables—Student Sample (*N* = 532)

Variable	Owned handgun		Owned Sawed-off shotgun	Carried gun routinely
	Auto/semiauto	Revolver		
	Beta Coefficients			
Criminal activity	.608	.435	1.373*	1.663*
Status enhancement	.198	.329*	.335	.230
Need for protection	.755*	.762*	.220	.601*
Age	.062	.025	.106	.043
Race ethnicity[a]				
Black	.665	−.012	−.218	1.152
Hispanic	−.488	−.811	−1.666*	.150
Site[b]				
California	.615	.441	8.808	1.900*
Illinois	.669	.533	7.746	.855
Louisiana	.540	−.212	7.724	1.527*
Constant	−4.746*	−2.818	−12.569*	−6.333*
Model χ^2 (df = 9)	58.973*	54.156*	41.518*	63.444*

* $p < .05$.
[a] "Other" omitted.
[b] New Jersey omitted.

able has been added for the inmate sample: having fired a gun at someone. No comparable item exists for the student sample.

Criminal activity is measured, for inmates, in terms of involvement in armed robbery and, for students, in terms of use of a weapon to commit a crime. Status enhancement is measured for both samples in terms of agreement that "In my crowd, if you don't have a gun, people don't respect you." Need for protection is measured for both samples in terms of whether or not the respondent has been threatened or shot at with a gun; this item, more than any other individual item common to both samples appears to indicate level of danger in the respondent's social world (see Chapter 2). Findings are displayed in Table 4.10 and 4.11.

Net of the effects of site and sociodemographic variables, and net of the effects of each other, criminal activity and need for protection are linked consistently and positively to the gun-related activities of the inmate respondents. Those who have committed armed robbery and those who have been threatened or shot at with a gun are more likely to own handguns and sawed-off shotguns, more likely to carry guns routinely, and more likely to have fired a gun at someone. Status enhancement clearly is not related to these behaviors.

Net of the effects of the same variables, a somewhat different picture emerges for students regarding criminality and the need for protection.

Students who have committed crimes with weapons are more likely to own sawed-off shotguns and to carry guns routinely. They are *not* more likely to own handguns.[11] Conversely, those who have been threatened with a gun or shot at are more likely to own a handgun but *not* to own a sawed-off shotgun or to carry a gun routinely. Transport of guns and ownership of sawed-off shotguns thus seems a function of participation in crime and has nothing to do with protection for students. But handgun ownership is related to the need for protection independent of criminal involvement. As well, status enhancement seems to influence ownership of a revolver though not an automatic or semiautomatic handgun or sawed-off shotgun, and not the carrying of a gun.[12]

Summary

All the evidence reviewed here intimates that, among the juveniles we studied, the odds of surviving in a hostile environment were better if one were armed than if not. We commented in Chapter 2 on the exceptional rates of crime, violence, and gun activity that plagued the communities from which our respondents (both groups) were drawn. We noted the significant percentages of respondents in both samples who felt that shooting another person was justified under circumstances that conventional society would not deem appropriate.[13] In such an environment, juveniles in both samples, and especially in the inmate sample, ran significant risks of physical injury and intimidation in their streets and neighborhoods. Indeed, substantial numbers had been shot, shot at, stabbed, or otherwise wounded in their young lives; even more had been threatened with physical violence at one or another time. If their enemies and even perfect strangers possessed the weapons and mentality that allowed them to take a life quickly and easily from a distance, our respondents likely reasoned that arming themselves was necessary. Even the perpetrators of violence faced significant risks from their victims and rivals; to illustrate, 70 percent of the inmate sample had been "scared off, shot at, wounded, or captured" by an armed victim at least once in their lives.

We hesitate to label the juvenile's use of a gun in crime as peripheral to the possession of a gun, since so many of the inmate respondents had used guns for crime. We suspect instead that any gun that is procured for protection (or status) is viewed as well as *potentially* instrumental in committing crimes. Unfortunately, the implications of these results are not encouraging. The perception that one's very survival depends on being armed makes a weapon a necessity at nearly any cost. Attempts to reduce juvenile gun-related crime through threat of criminal justice sanctions can hardly be expected to produce results if a juvenile "must" have a gun to survive, and crimes are committed with guns because they happen to be in the youth's possession. Gun-related crime (though not necessarily all weapon-related crime) then likely will decrease only when juveniles are convinced that they do not have to carry guns for protection.

Notes

1. Items used to assess weapon and gun use in crimes included the following: "How old were you the first time you committed a crime with a weapon?" "with a gun?" "Before you came to this facility about how often did you use a weapon to commit a crime?" (Response categories included "almost every day," "a few times each week," "a few times each month," "a few times a year," "only once or twice in my life," "never.") Regarding specific gun-related crimes, respondents were asked: "Did you ever get a gun specifically to use in committing crimes?" "Have you ever actually fired a gun at someone?" "Have you ever committed a crime while armed with a revolver (regular handgun)?" "with a military-style automatic or semiautomatic rifle?" "with an automatic or semiautomatic handgun?" "Have you ever fired a gun during a crime?" (Response categories included "yes," "no.")

2. By comparison, according to the official court records of a sample of 203 violent adjudicated delinquents from Boston, Newark, Memphis, and Detroit in the early 1980s, 43 percent had threatened an adult with a weapon, 45 percent had used a weapon "to get something," and 23 percent had shot someone (Fagan et al. 1986).

3. No specific item in our survey asked students about this behavior. Our estimate derives first from asking students if they carried a weapon and, if so, from their rating of the importance ("not at all," "somewhat," "very") of the following statement as a reason for carrying a weapon: "Sometimes I use weapons to commit crimes." Students who rated the statement as somewhat or very important (9 percent) are assumed to have used a weapon in a crime. By comparison, Altschuler and Brounstein (1991) report that, of a sample of 387 Washington, D.C. minority, inner-city ninth and tenth graders, 11 percent had used a weapon to threaten someone, 9 percent had robbed someone, 11 percent had assaulted an adult, and 5 percent had shot, stabbed, or killed someone.

4. We exclude from discussion here possession of hunting rifles, derringers, zip guns, and so forth. Fewer respondents owned such guns, and such guns are generally not associated with criminal activity.

5.   Theft and arrest history are relatively strongly related ($r = .402$). Commission of a crime with a weapon is considerably less related to arrest history ($r = .160$) and somewhat more strongly related to theft ($r = .233$).

6.   We repeated the analysis with those who reported having committed armed robbery and obtained identical results. The item regarding being armed with a gun during commission of a crime asked: "When you committed your crimes, about how often were you armed with a gun?" (Response categories were "always," "usually," "sometimes," and "never.") The item regarding reasons for carrying a weapon during commission of a crime stated: "There are many different reasons why a person like yourself might decide to carry a weapon while doing a crime. Read over the following reasons and, for each one, indicate how important the reason was to you in your decision to carry a weapon." The list of reasons included:

"There's always a chance the victim would be armed."

"You have to be ready to defend yourself."

"If you have a weapon, your victim doesn't put up a fight, and that way you don't have to hurt them."

"I felt I might need a weapon to escape."

"People just don't mess with you when you have a weapon."

For each item, respondents were asked to check "Very Important," "Somewhat Important," or "Not Important."

7.   This same pattern is borne out in an examination of the correlation coefficients describing the relationships among the reasons to bear arms. The highest coefficient ($r = .415$) emerged between the perceived need to defend oneself during a crime and the concern that a victim might be armed. The possible need for a weapon to facilitate an escape was also related to these two items ($r = .300$ and $.310$, respectively). The items pertaining to intimidation through a weapon were more highly related than either was to two of the other three reasons in the question ($r = .302$). The exception pertained to the relationship between the perceived need to defend oneself during a crime and the view that a weapon discourages a victim from resisting an offender.

8.   The specific item stated: "How likely were you to carry a gun with you in each of the following situations?" For each situation (see Table 4.7 for the possibilities), respondents could check "very likely," "somewhat likely," or "not too likely."

9.   This item was asked of each respondent who had obtained a military-style weapon, a handgun, or a rifle or shotgun. Specifically, it stated: "Look over the list of reasons below and circle the number that comes closest to saying how *important* that reason was to you when you got your most recent rifle or shotgun." For each possible response (see

Table 4.8 for possibilities), respondents could reply, "very important," "somewhat important," or "not important."

10.   Specifically, the inmates were asked: "Have you ever fired a gun in any of the following situations?" For each situation (see Table 4.9 for possibilities), response categories included "never," "once," "a few times," and "many times."

11.   When missing cases are included in the analysis, the relationship between criminal activity and ownership of both types of handgun becomes significant.

12.   When the alternative measure of carrying a gun is employed (i.e., no carrying vs. any carrying), the relationship between status enhancement and carrying is significant.

13.   Recall that we asked respondents the extent to which they agreed or disagreed that it is acceptable to shoot someone to get something you want, to shoot someone who hurts or insults you, to shoot someone who hurts or insults your family (asked of inmates only), and to shoot some guy if he doesn't belong in your neighborhood. For each item, respondents who expressed agreement reported higher levels of gun possession and carrying. Though the differences were less pronounced among those who had committed robbery, they were generally significant. Among those who had never fired a gun at anyone, agreement or disagreement with a statement was not associated with level of gun possession and carrying; among those who had, the opposite was true. Overall, it appears that personal antivictimization policy in an environment in which people are willing to shoot strangers or those who insult them reduces to avoiding the streets almost entirely or to be armed when out.

5

YOUTH, DRUGS, AND GUNS

It's the dope, man, it has tore the 'hood up. . . . But De wasn't like the others. He cared about the homies and put a lot of the li'l homies down with crack and straps. He got caught up in some bullshit and was gaffled for two hot ones. [*Translation*: Drug dealing has caused neighborhood instability. But De took care of the neighborhood guys and supplied a lot of the younger neighborhood guys with crack and guns. Unfortunately, he is now awaiting trial for two murders.]

—quoted in K. Scott, *Monster: The Autobiography of an L.A. Gang Member*

As we noted in Chapter 1, a presumed link between drug activity (use and sales) and the possession, carrying, and use of firearms is a relative staple of governmental and media analyses of crime and violence by youth in the United States. Military-style automatic firearms are afforded special attention as the weapons of choice of drug traffickers. Popular perceptions aside, little research has been conducted concerning drug use and weapons generally, much less concerning drug use and firearms specifically. Only somewhat more is known empirically about the relation of firearms to drug distribution.

In the present chapter, we examine a number of issues: links between hard drug use and gun-related activity and between "heavy" drug use and gun-related activity; the association between drug distribution and firearms; and the interrelationships among drug use and sales, predatory violence, and firearms.

Prior Research on Drugs and Guns

Much about drug use and weapons is *assumed* by virtue of possible links between hard-drug abuse (heroin, cocaine, crack) and predatory crime. Students of the issue generally conclude that such relationships exist, but that the direction of causation and its application to all

75

forms of drug users and predation and across levels of addiction are unclear (Chaiken and Johnson 1988; Gentry 1995). As well, much of the link between predatory crime and drug abuse is confounded by relationships between each of these variables and such factors as IQ level, school record, and inadequate parental supervision (Blumstein et al. 1985).

Fourteen percent of juveniles incarcerated for the crime of robbery in long-term, state-operated facilities in 1987 had committed their crimes while under the influence of drugs; another 31 percent were under the combined influence of drugs and alcohol (Beck, Kline, and Greenfeld 1988). Yet, there is only limited evidence that ingestion of substances is a direct, pharmacological cause of aggression (Fagan and Weis 1990:241). An indirect association between drug abuse and violence, primarily through criminal attempts to support a habit, is more likely. Robbery, presumably accomplished through use of some form of weapon, is apparently not uncommon among serious users of hard drugs and especially among those whose addictions require daily or multiple daily use (Johnson, Williams, Dei, and Sanabria 1990:42). Among heroin users with a high rate of predatory crime, intensity of offending seems to vary directly with intensity of drug use (Anglin and Speckart 1986; Nurco, Hanlon, Kinlock, and Dusczinski 1988).

Beyond relationships inferred from links between predatory crime and drug abuse, empirically documented associations between abuse and weapons activity are scarce. Altschuler and Brounstein (1991) report statistically significant associations between the carrying and use of weapons and the level of drug use in a sample of inner-city youth. Thirty-one percent of those who used but did not sell drugs had carried a concealed weapon; 14 percent had threatened another person with a weapon. Fifteen percent of the whole sample reported threatening another person with a weapon while under the influence of drugs; 13 percent did so in order to obtain drugs. Callahan and Rivara (1992) find that 20 percent of the students in their Seattle sample of eleventh graders who had used cocaine also owned a gun. Lizotte et al. (1994) report that 60 percent of their Rochester adolescent respondents who owned guns for protective purposes used drugs other than alcohol; this compared to 48 and 26 percent of the respondents who owned guns for sporting reasons or who owned no guns, respectively.

Particular public concern has been directed at the link between violence and drug trafficking. Importantly, a strong relationship between drug use and drug sales should not be assumed: drug users and drug distributors are not necessarily the same persons (Altschuler and Brounstein 1991). Not uncommonly, for example, gangs engaged in drug sales strongly discourage drug use among members (Chin 1990;

Cooper 1987; Mieczkowski 1986; Stumphauzer, Veloz, and Aiken 1981). In this light, there seems considerable consensus that much of drug-related violence today is linked to the distribution rather than the abuse of drugs (Chaiken and Chaiken 1990; Johnson et al. 1990; Wright and Devine 1994). Altschuler and Brounstein (1991) find higher levels of personal crime, weapons carrying, and weapons use among drug-selling youth than among drug-using youth (though the latter are higher in property crime). Callahan and Rivara (1992) report that 32 percent of their sample of high school students who had sold drugs had owned a handgun; only 4 percent of those who had not sold drugs had owned such a firearm. Lizotte et al. (1994) find that, among Rochester public school students, nearly one-third of those who owned guns for other than sporting reasons also had sold drugs.

It is generally thought that drug-selling organizations recruit physically violent employees who may themselves seek out such organizations (Chaiken and Chaiken 1982). As well, persons who sell drugs publicly (as opposed to private selling among friends) appear to commit predatory offenses at higher rates than do persons who commit such offenses but do not sell drugs (Chaiken and Chaiken 1990; Williams and Kornblum 1985). This is the case even for drug sellers without a use habit. Pertinent to the topic of this report, drugs sales have also been linked to substantially higher rates of armed robbery by urban youth (Fagan and Weis 1990). Fagan (1992:118) reports that robberies and assaults increase to the extent that offenders move from nonsales to independent sales to group sales of drugs.

The above notwithstanding, most of the violence involved in drug trafficking seems systemic (Fagan and Chin 1990; Goldstein 1985). Weapons are used to intimidate workers, competitors, and neighborhood residents. Such intimidation by persons with little training in the use of firearms often produces injuries to innocent bystanders (Johnson et al. 1990:35, 38). However, beyond speculation that rates of violence by drug sellers appear to have risen due to increased availability of automatic firearms (Kleiman and Smith 1990:91; U.S. Senate, Committee on the Judiciary 1991), little actually is known about links between drug trafficking and such weapons.

Drugs and Guns in the Present Samples

It is clear from the above review that little has occurred in the way of a systematic assessment of the gun possession and gun use profiles of young persons involved in the use and distribution of drugs. We are able to shed some light on the issue. Both inmate and student respondents were asked the frequency of their use of heroin, cocaine, and crack—during the "year or two" preceding confinement for the inmates and during the past "year or two" for the students (see Chapter 2). Forty-three percent of the inmates had used cocaine, 25 percent crack, and 21 percent heroin. Forty-seven percent reported use of at least one of these drugs, and 53 percent of the inmates had *not* used hard drugs at all in the year or two preceding confinement. Thirteen percent of the inmates had hard-drug use scores (sum of the frequencies of each type of drug used; scores ranged from 0 to 12) of no more than 2 (two drugs once each or one drug "a few times"), and 34 percent had scores of 3 or higher. One-quarter of the inmates were "heavy" drug users (using heroin, cocaine, or crack, individually or in combination, "many times" or "almost all the time" during the year or two preceding confinement)—40 percent of whom were cocaine and 39 percent of whom were polydrug users.

Four percent of the student sample had used heroin, 6 percent cocaine, and 5 percent crack. Seven percent reported use of at least one of these drugs, and 93 percent of the students had *not* used hard drugs at all in the previous year or two. Two percent of the students had hard-drug use scores of no more than 2 (two drugs once each or one drug "a few times"). Five percent had scores of 3 or higher. Five percent of the students were "heavy" drug users (71 percent of whom were polydrug users).

In addition to questions regarding drug use, respondents were asked to describe their involvement in drug sales. Three-quarters of the inmates had sold drugs (48 percent had sold but not used drugs; 25 percent had both used and sold drugs). Eighteen percent of the students had sold drugs (16 percent had sold but not used drugs; 2 percent had both used and sold drugs).

Drug Use and Gun Activity

To gain a sense of the potential link between drug use and gun activity, we rely upon responses regarding those guns considered most associated with drugs, crime, and violence: revolvers, automatic or semiautomatic handguns, military-style automatic or semiautomatic rifles, and regular or sawed-off shotguns (see discussion in Chapter 4). We examine as well possible links between routine gun carrying (carrying "all of the time" or "most of the time") and drug use and, for the inmates only, the relation of drug use to having fired a gun at someone.

The findings presented in Table 5.1 make apparent, first of all, that

Table 5.1. Inmates' Firearm Possession by Hard-Drug Use Score

| Firearm activity[b] | Hard drug use score[a] (%) | | | | | (N) |
	0 (N = 365)	1 (N = 23)	2 (N = 66)	3 (N = 51)	4+ (N = 182)	
Possession						
No gun	22	9	14	14	13	(681)
Revolver	58	61	56	59	58	(681)
Automatic or semiautomatic handgun	53	52	46	61	57	(681)
Military-style automatic or semiautomatic rifle	35	35	36	24	35	(681)
Regular shotgun[c]	32	30	41	41	47	(681)
Sawed-off shotgun	46	48	56	55	54	(681)
Owned 3 or more guns	62	64	61	65	66	(675)
Carrying and use						
Carried gun routinely	51	65	48	44	56	(666)
Fired at someone	72	82	74	74	79	(668)

[a] See text for measurement details. N in parentheses for hard-drug use score refers to distribution prior to cross-tabulation with gun possession items.
[b] Item refers to gun possession immediately prior to confinement.
[c] p < .01; all other relationships described in this table are not statistically significant.

substantial numbers of *nonusers* among the inmate sample engaged in all the behaviors in question. That important point made, it is also clear that there is little relationship between hard-drug use score and gun activity among the inmates. The tendency to have owned a regular shotgun generally increased with level of drug use. However, no statistically significant association emerged concerning ownership of revolvers, automatic or semiautomatic handguns, or military-style automatic and semiautomatic rifles and an inmate's hard-drug use score. Nor was drug use related to number of guns owned or to the routine carrying of guns. Indeed, carrying and using guns were most common among those with hard-drug use scores of 1.

The findings presented in Table 5.2 indicate that moderate numbers of *nonusers* among the students engaged in all the firearms-related behaviors in question. As with the inmates, apart from differences between student non-drug users and drug users, there is little relationship between hard-drug use score and gun activity. The tendency to have owned a regular shotgun *decreased* with level of drug use. Yet, no statistically significant association emerged concerning ownership of revolvers, automatic or semiautomatic handguns, or military-style automatic and semiautomatic rifles and hard-drug use score. Drug use was related to the routine carrying of guns. However, as with possession of a rifle, carrying a gun was more common among students with hard-drug use scores below 4.

Table 5.2. Students' Firearm Possession by Hard-Drug Use Score

	Hard-drug use score[a] (%)			
Possession: firearm type[b]	0 (N = 538)	1-3 (N = 15)	4+ (N = 27)	(N)
No gun	73	50	48	(555)
Revolver	13	15	30	(555)
Automatic or semiautomatic handgun	14	32	30	(555)
Military-style automatic or semiautomatic rifle	5	7	9	(555)
Regular shotgun[c]	7	36	22	(555)
Sawed-off shotgun	5	21	22	(555)
Owned 3 or more guns	11	29	30	(567)
Carries gun routinely[c]	8	43	26	(535)

[a] See text for measurement details. N in parentheses for hard drug use score refers to distribution prior to cross-tabulations with gun possession items.
[b] Item refers to gun possession at present time.
[c] $p < .05$. All other relationships described in this table are not statistically significant.

Table 5.3. Inmates' Firearm Possession by "Heavy" Drug Use

| Firearm activity[b] | Type of "heavy" drug use[a] (%) | | | | | |
	None (N = 504)	Cocaine (N = 72)	Heroin (N = 21)	Crack (N = 17)	Poly (N = 73)	(N)
Possession						
No gun	19	14	14	14	16	(681)
Revolver	58	55	57	62	60	(681)
Automatic or semiautomatic handgun	52	55	64	57	60	(681)
Military-style automatic or semiautomatic rifle	34	34	14	19	41	(681)
Regular shotgun[c]	35	44	21	43	55	(681)
Sawed-off shotgun	48	62	43	48	55	(681)
Owned 3 or more guns	61	65	71	67	74	(675)
Carrying and use						
Carried gun routinely	51	55	36	50	67	(666)
Fired at someone	73	76	71	81	79	(670)

[a] See text for measurement details. N in parentheses for heavy drug use score refers to distribution prior to cross-tabulation with gun possession items. Polydrug users include no members of the remaining categories.
[b] Item refers to gun possession immediately prior to confinement.
[c] $p < .01$; all other relationships described in this table are not statistically significant.

As previously indicated, it is possible that relationships between drug use and gun possession and use may be more prominent among and may vary across different types of "heavy" drug users. The findings displayed in Table 5.3 bear on this question. Among the inmate respondents, gun possession generally was not a function of "heavy" drug use; the difference between non–"heavy" users and "heavy" users was minimal. Only regarding possession of a regular shotgun was a statistically significant relationship apparent ("heavy" polydrug users were especially more likely to possess such a gun). However, momentarily ignoring the lack of statistical significance across *all* categories and focusing on the extremes, we encounter some differences in gun possession and carrying. "Heavy" polydrug users, for example, were more than twice as likely than "heavy" heroin users to possess a military-style rifle. "Heavy" cocaine users greatly exceeded "heavy" heroin users in possession of a sawed-off shotgun. "Heavy" polydrug users nearly doubled "heavy" heroin users in the percentage carrying guns routinely. To the extent that patterns arise regarding "heavy" use and gun possession then, they seem most likely to involve heroin and polydrug users.

Though the number of "heavy" drug users among the student respondents limits interpretation of the findings somewhat (in that it prohibits assessment of relationships between *type* of "heavy" use and gun possession), it is fairly clear from the results displayed in Table 5.4 that gun possession was associated with "heavy" drug use; the difference between student non–"heavy" users and "heavy" users was substantial. It appears that, despite the findings of no linear relationship between

Table 5.4. Students' Firearm Possession by "Heavy" Drug Use[a]

	"Heavy" drug use[b] (%)		
Possession: firearm type[c]	No (N = 553)	Yes (N = 30)	(N)
No gun	72	55	(555)
Revolver	13	72	(555)
Automatic or semiautomatic handgun	15	72	(555)
Military-style automatic or semiautomatic rifle	11	88	(555)
Regular shotgun	8	77	(555)
Sawed-off shotgun	6	83	(555)
Owned 3 or more guns	12	77	(567)
Carried guns routinely	10	72	(535)

[a] All relationships reported in this table are statistically significant.
[b] See text for measurement details. N in parentheses for heavy drug use refers to distribution prior to cross-tabulation with gun possession items.
[c] Item refers to gun possession at present time.

hard-drug score and gun possession among students, there was a point at which gun activity increased among users. Those who were involved in "heavy" use were more likely to possess guns than were those who were not. We suspect that the world of the student "heavy" drug user differed considerably from that of the student who had not become or was on his way to becoming a "heavy" user.

Drug Distribution and Gun Activity

Prior research points to drug sellers as highly involved in violence, this primarily by virtue of the systemic violence attendant to their trade and perhaps because the trade attracts particularly violent participants. The issue of whether or not inmate drug sellers were more or less likely to possess or use guns than were nonsellers is addressed in Table 5.5.

In Table 5.5, respondents are divided into four categories: (1) those who neither used nor sold drugs, (2) those who used but did not sell drugs, (3) those who used and sold drugs, and (4) those who sold but did not use drugs. It is clear quickly that sellers of drugs among the inmates were far more likely to have owned every type of weapon in question, to have possessed three or more guns, to have carried a gun routinely, and to have fired a gun at someone than were those who neither used nor sold drugs. In most cases, the percentage of sellers (i.e., sold but did not use drugs) possessing, carrying, or using firearms was at least double the percentage of those who did not use or sell drugs. The findings (columns 2 and 3) also indicate a progression in gun activity as inmates moved from drug use to both using and selling; the one exception concerns possession of military-style weapons. It is apparent also (columns 3 and 4) that sellers who did not use drugs were more likely than those who combined use and sales to possess and carry firearms; the only exceptions pertained to possession of unaltered and altered shotguns (the latter separated by only two percentage points). But sellers who did not use drugs were not more likely to have fired a gun at someone.

Essentially the same disparities occur when we look solely at the "heavy" drug users among the inmates (Table 5.6). Dividing "heavy" users into two groups—users only and users and sellers—we find that users who were involved in sales were more likely to possess a gun generally, to possess an automatic or semiautomatic handgun, to own at least three guns, and to carry a gun routinely. Differences pertaining to other possession and use items were not statistically significant.

Regarding firearm possession and drug selling among the student

Table 5.5. Inmates' Firearm Possession by Drug Use and Sales[a,b]

Firearm activity	No use/no sale (%) (N = 113)	Use only (%) (N = 85)	Use and sale (%) (N = 324)	Sale only (%) (N = 173)	(N)
Possession					
No gun	43	29	12	9	(686)
Revolver	37	49	57	69	(686)
Automatic or semiautomatic handgun	29	45	58	66	(686)
Military-style automatic or semiautomatic rifle	18	28	29	45	(686)
Regular shotgun	20	34	45	39	(686)
Sawed-off shotgun	25	31	57	59	(686)
Owned 3 or more guns	38	50	66	75	(634)
Carrying and use					
Carried gun routinely	29	42	57	66	(671)
Fired at someone	45	63	85	78	(672)

[a] All relationships reported in this table are statistically significant.
[b] Measurement described in text. Firearm possession and carrying refers to practices immediately prior to incarceration. N in parentheses for use or sales refers to distribution prior to cross-tabulation with gun possession items.

Table 5.6. Inmates' Firearm Possession by "Heavy" Drug Use and Sales

Firearm activity	"Heavy" drug use and use/sales[a] (%)		(N)
	"Heavy" use only (N = 27)	"Heavy" use and sales (N = 154)	
Possession			
No gun[b]	23	11	(173)
Revolver	54	60	(173)
Automatic or semiautomatic handgun[b]	44	65	(173)
Military-style automatic or semiautomatic rifle	28	36	(173)
Regular shotgun	40	49	(173)
Sawed-off shotgun	46	60	(173)
Owned 3 or more guns[b]	58	74	(164)
Carrying and use			
Carried gun routinely[b]	41	65	(174)
Fired at someone	73	80	(176)

[a] Measurement described in text. Firearm possession and carrying refers to practices at the time of incarceration. N in parentheses for use or sales refers to distribution prior to cross-tabulation with gun possession items.
[b] $p < .05$.

Table 5.7. Students' Firearm Possession by Drug Use and Sales[a]

Firearm possession/carrying	Drug use and drug sales[b] (%)			(N)
	No use/ No sale (N = 446)	Use/use and sale (N = 21)	Sale only (N = 93)	
No gun[c]	80	28	38	(539)
Revolver	8	38	32	(539)
Automatic or semiautomatic handgun[c]	8	33	45	(539)
Military-style automatic or semiautomatic rifle	4	14	11	(539)
Regular shotgun[c]	5	38	16	(539)
Sawed-off shotgun	3	23	14	(539)
Owned 3 or more guns	8	28	28	(550)
Carried guns routinely[c]	5	19	19	(525)

[a] Measurement described in text. Firearm possession and carrying refer to practices at the time of the survey.
[b] N in parentheses for use or sales refers to distribution prior to cross-tabulation with gun possession items.
[c] $p < .05$.

sample, respondents who were drug sellers were indeed highly active relative to students who neither used nor sold drugs, though differences were less pronounced than among the inmate population. In an attempt to sort out the effects of using drugs from selling drugs, in Table 5.7 we have separated users and user/sellers (a small number of respondents) from those who were nonusing sellers. Interestingly, respondents who both used and sold drugs exceeded those who sold drugs only both in possession of firearms generally and in possession of regular shotguns. Yet, in line with public perceptions of drug dealers as gun oriented, we found those in the business of selling drugs—that is, those who sold but did not use drugs—more likely to possess an automatic or semiautomatic handgun and to carry a firearm routinely.[1]

Drugs, Predation, and Gun Activity

According to the literature on crime and drug activity, levels of predatory crime, especially armed robbery, appear to increase with movement into drug sales. The issue of interest here involves differences between drug sellers who commit predatory crimes and those who do not in the *types* of firearm possessed, number of guns possessed, the practice of routinely carrying guns, and, for inmates, firing a gun at someone. To provide an answer, we examine differences between subsets of inmates uninvolved and involved in drug activity: nonusers/nonsellers (no involvement in drug activity), users (who did not sell drugs), user/sellers (who used and sold drugs), and sellers (who did not use drugs). For each category, predatory criminal activity is measured in terms of whether or not the respondent had ever committed an armed robbery.

The findings reported in Table 5.8 indicate that, with few exceptions, inmate robbers exceeded nonrobbers in firearm activity across all drug user/seller subgroups. This was especially the case (using statistical significance as the criterion) for drug sellers who did not use drugs (column 4). Notably, however, the highest levels of gun involvement occurred among those who both used *and* sold drugs. The major exceptions to the pattern pertain to possession of regular shotguns and military-style automatic or semiautomatic rifles. Robbers did not differ from nonrobbers in possession of such weapons across the categories of those without drug activity, those who used but did not sell drugs, and those who used and sold drugs (columns 1, 2, and 3). Beyond this, the only nonsignificant differences appeared regarding possession of automatic or semiautomatic handguns by nonusers/nonsellers and the ownership of three or more guns by users who did not sell.

Table 5.8. Drug Users' and Sellers' Firearm Possession by Involvement in Armed Robbery[a]

	Non-robber/robber (NR/R) (%)			
Firearm activity	No use/no sale (N = 107)	Use only (N = 84)	Use and sale (N = 310)	Sale only (N = 168)
Possession				
No gun	52/17*	40/15*	15/3*	25/5*
Revolver	29/60*	40/62*	62/75*	48/63*
Automatic or semi-automatic handgun	25/40	36/56*	58/74*	44/68*
Military-style automatic or semiautomatic rifle	16/23	24/35	40/51	18/37*
Regular shotgun	18/23	36/32	35/44	32/56*
Sawed-off shotgun	21/40*	20/47*	49/70*	43/70*
Owned 3 or more guns	29/63*	43/62	66/86*	42/82*
Carrying and use				
Carried gun routinely	17/52*	30/59*	58/74*	44/66*
Fired at someone	34/76*	52/78*	78/96*	61/89*

[a] Measurement described in text. Firearm possession and carrying refers to practices immediately prior to incarceration.
* $p < .05$. Statistical significance refers to differences *within* drug user and drug seller pairs.

The issue at hand becomes somewhat more cloudy when we examine it utilizing data collected from the high school students. Predatory criminal activity among students is measured in terms of whether the respondent had ever committed a crime with a weapon. Since the number of students who both used and sold drugs is too small to permit fully answering the question at hand, we limit our analysis to respondents who had sold but not used drugs.[2] We note, however, that, for some gun possession categories, users and user/sellers reported higher involvement than did nonuser/sellers.

The findings reported in Table 5.9 indicate that, somewhat surprisingly, student drug sellers who had committed crimes with weapons were statistically no more likely than those who had not to possess firearms in general, regular and automatic or semiautomatic handguns, military-style firearms, and regular shotguns. Drug sellers who had committed crimes with weapons were, however, statistically more likely to own sawed-off shotguns, to possess three or more guns, and to carry guns routinely.

Given that these are cross-sectional data, we cannot know whether either sample's predator–drug sellers' involvement in firearm activity reflected sellers' choice to commit predatory crimes or predatory offenders' choice to sell drugs. The findings point generally to the conclusion that the most dangerous *inmates* (in terms of firearm activity) in our sample were those who combined robbery with drug sales (including those who robbed and used and sold drugs)—see columns 3 and 4 of Table 5.8. Looking only at columns 2 and 4 of Table 5.8 (i.e., looking at users only *versus* sellers only) it is clear that robbery raised the odds of firearm activity among drug sellers though it is still not known whether drug sales attracted or produced such relatively more dangerous persons. However, across most variables, the highest gun activity levels were recorded by robbers who engaged in both drug use and sales. This suggests what is likely a less organized and structured, more opportunistic involvement in all three activities; this offender profile approximates the public stereotype of the "urban marauder" that fuels crime fears and informs anticrime policy.

These same conclusions are less apparent regarding the *student* drug sellers who committed predatory crimes. They more likely owned more guns and carried guns more often; yet the quality of their arsenal, with the exception of sawed-off shotguns, was little different from that of sellers who did not commit predatory crimes. On the one hand, we could argue that since drug sellers already were better armed than non–drug sellers (see Table 5.7), their need to arm themselves further for predation was low. On the other hand, the findings from the inmate sample should lend themselves to the same logic but do not. It may be that the forms of predation practiced by the inmate sellers differed from

Table 5.9.   Student Drug Sellers' Firearm Possession by Involvement in Crimes Committed with Weapons[a]

	Committed crime with a weapon (%) (N = 80)	
Firearm possession/carrying	Yes	No
No gun	33	39
Revolver	27	34
Automatic or semiautomatic handgun	53	45
Military-style automatic or semiautomatic rifle	20	10
Regular shotgun	33	15
Sawed-off shotgun	33	9*
Owned 3 or more guns	53	23*
Carried guns routinely	57	28*

[a] Measurement described in text. Firearm possession and carrying refers to practices at the time of the survey.
* $p < .05$.

or were done more frequently than those by student sellers. The inmate "urban marauder" may have been so active that he accumulated, carried, and used nearly every type of gun more than did his counterpart among the students. The latter may have been a far less active predator who needed somewhat less an arsenal.

Multivariate Considerations

As in the previous two chapters, we have employed logistic regression models to sort out the relationship between drug activity and gun activity independent of the effects of sociodemographic characteristics, site, and motivations for gun possession. In the present instance, drug use is measured in terms of hard-drug use score. Drug selling is mea-

Table 5.10. Logistic Regression of Firearm-Related Activities on Motivational, Drug Activity, Sociodemographic, and Site Variables—Inmate Sample ($N = 530$)

	Beta coefficients				
	Owned handgun		Owned sawed-off shotgun	Carried gun routinely	Fired gun at someone
Variable	Auto/ semiauto	Revolver			
Criminal activity	.230*	.209*	.278*	.292*	.413*
Status enhancement	−.034	−.101	.070	.128	−.047
Prior gun threats	.779*	.659*	.590*	1.038*	1.152*
Drug use	−.015	−.107*	−.037	.012	−.061
Drug sales	.526*	.454	.899*	.576*	.627
Age	.034	−.008	.014	−.089	.005
Race/ethnicity[a]					
Black	−.102	−.376	−.367	.073	.343
Hispanic	−.147	−.086	−.067	−.109	.301
White	−.154	−.349	−.446	−.399	−.070
City Size	.014	.013	−.048	.002	.031
Site[b]					
California	−.057	.741*	.404	.731*	.766*
Illinois	−.515	.847*	.393	.813	.998
Louisiana	.501	1.038*	.674	.354	.160
Constant	−2.309	−1.609	−2.267	−1.706	−2.350
Model χ^2 (df = 13)	116.036*	99.379*	111.431*	173.244*	177.923*

* $p < .05$.
[a] "Other" omitted.
[b] New Jersey omitted.

Table 5.11. Logistic Regression of Firearm-Related Activities on Motivational, Drug Activity, Sociodemographic, and Site Variables—Student Sample (N = 465)

	Beta coefficients			
	Owned handgun		Owned	Carried gun
Variable	Auto/semiauto	Revolver	sawed-off shotgun	routinely
Criminal activity	.570	−.090	1.545*	1.749*
Status enhancement	.084	.297	.297	.024
Prior gun threats	.559*	.575*	−.074	.315
Drug use	−.045	−.005	.034	−.016
Drug sales	1.855*	1.052*	1.309*	1.694*
Age	.112	.019	.238	.111
Race/ethnicity[a]				
Black	.184	.079	−.319	.874
Hispanic	−.486	−.445	−1.690	.115
Site[b]				
California	.947	.447	8.030	1.851*
Illinois	1.214*	.711	7.855	.758
Louisiana	.755	.064	6.885	1.409*
Constant	−5.650	−3.748	−14.829	−7.112
Model χ^2 (df = 11)	95.607*	51.645*	47.887*	73.508*

* $p < .05$.
[a] "Other" omitted.
[b] New Jersey omitted.

sured in terms of whether of not a respondent had sold drugs in the last year or two or, for inmates, in the year or two preceding confinement (see Chapter 2).

The findings displayed in Tables 5.10 (inmates) and 5.11 (students) bear out fairly straightforwardly those discussed above. At the bivariate level, the link between drug use and gun-related activity was not wholly clear. Here, independent of the effects of other variables, drug use is linked only to the ownership of a revolver among inmates, and this relationship is negative. Otherwise, the firearm-related behaviors of interest are not influenced by drug use for either inmates and students. Drug sales by inmates is related to their possession of all but revolvers, to carrying guns routinely, and to having fired a gun at someone. For the students, drug selling influences all of the behaviors we have examined.[3]

Summary

Exploring the possibility of a relationship between drug activity and possession and use of firearms, we noted early in this chapter that substantial numbers of *nonusers* of drugs in the inmate sample and moderate numbers of *nonusers* in the student sample engaged in all forms of gun activity examined here. We found little by way of a progressive, linear relationship between either hard-drug use score and gun possession, including number of guns owned and the routine carrying of guns. We did find, however, that when we compared nonusers with users of drugs and, among students but not among inmates, non-"heavy" users with "heavy" users, significant differences in levels of gun activity did appear. As well, when we compared users who did not sell drugs with users who did, the latter generally displayed higher levels of gun possession, carrying, and use. Drug selling clearly increased levels of gun activity among the respondents. Finally, drug users and sellers who also committed predatory crimes exceeded nonpredator counterparts in involvement in most forms of gun activity, though this was truer of the inmates than of the students.

There is clearly no certainty that relationships between drug activity and gun activity are *causal*. Most studies that report an association between delinquency or crime and drug use are careful to note "that the relationship may be spurious rather than causal" (Fagan 1990:184). An argument can easily be made that involvement in drugs leads one to possess, carry, and use firearms (Inciardi 1992:Ch. 5); recent longitudinal data analyses regarding gang members also point to such a conclusion (Thornberry, Krohn, Lizotte, and Wierschem 1993). It is obvious, however, that the use of drugs is not a *necessary* precondition of gun activity since nonusers in our sample were also heavily involved in all such activity.

It might also be argued that drug- and gun-related activity are both manifestations of an emerging normative structure, perhaps even a subculture, and that participation in this structure itself is the critical variable, not participation in any particular manifestation of it. The suggestion, in other words, is not that some youth become involved in drugs, which then leads them causally to guns, but that these youth get involved with peer structures and values whereby hanging out, getting high, and carrying and using guns become part and parcel of the daily routine of existence. In the same vein, Fagan has pointed out that "the association [between drug use and crime among youth] seems to be facilitated by the strength of involvement in peer social networks where drug use and delinquency are normative" (1990:184; see also White, Johnson, and Garrison 1985; White, Pandina, and LaGrange 1987). In sum, no one element may be causally prior to any other.

Whatever the causal links may be, the current cross-sectional findings suggest that the relationship between drug *use* and the possession, carrying, and use of guns is less direct than seems to be assumed by press and public—at least regarding seriously offending youth like those in the inmate sample. Dichotomizing drug users into those who neither use nor sell drugs and those who use but do not sell drugs produces evidence of *some* link between drug use and gun activity. However, we also find that gun activity does not increase in linear fashion with rises in level of drug use (except for students who seem to have crossed a threshold into "heavy" use). This might be explained by the likelihood that entry into drug use by a youth increases the probability that the youth associates more frequently with other juveniles who possess and carry guns and that the drug user at times feels sufficiently threatened in drug transactions to carry or use a gun. Beyond this, there is nothing to suggest that further movement into drug use increases directly the necessity to possess, carry, and use guns.

The case for a link between drug *sales* and gun activity is more compelling. Among the inmates, drug sellers (including nonusers and users of drugs) were especially likely to possess handguns (regular and automatic) and to carry and use firearms. Suggesting their involvement in a more dangerous business, drug sellers also were more likely to possess sawed-off shotguns. Essentially the same findings occurred among the student respondents, though we were unable to separate drug use and sales among the students as we were for the inmates.

The findings regarding predatory behavior among drug sellers were somewhat mixed, though generally supported the assertion of a link. It is clear that if gun activity is employed as a measure of dangerousness, those who both sold drugs and committed crimes with weapons were the most dangerous of the respondents in this investigation. In this sense, themes in the current literature find support in these findings.

Finally, the present results suggest that current policy aimed at deterring gun possession by drug sellers likely will produce little by way of reduction in their levels of gun activity. First, far more policy attention is given to military-style automatic rifles than is warranted by our findings. While ownership of such weapons was not infrequent, it is very clear that handguns (revolvers and automatic and semiautomatic sidearms) were the firearms of choice for respondents who were drug sellers. Sawed-off shotguns also were more prominent than military-style automatic or semiautomatic rifles. Second, the patterns of possession and use of guns found in this study suggest that drug sellers do not just happen upon firearms. Clearly, they find it in their interest to be armed and, in the face of a reduced supply of arms, probably would be willing to pay what is necessary for a gun.

In the coming chapter, we examine yet another element of the public perception of the gun problem: the relationship between gang membership and the various firearm-related activities of interest in this study.

We examine as well whether or not the findings regarding drug activity and gun-related activity hold once gang membership is controlled.

Notes

1.   The number of "heavy" users among students was too small to conduct a meaningful analysis of the relationship between selling and nonselling statuses and gun possession. To the extent that differences seemed likely, they pertained only to routine carrying of a firearm; to the extent that "heavy" users also engaged in drug sales, their likelihood of routine gun carrying rose dramatically.

2.   Recall that, of the total sample, only 9 percent had committed a crime with a weapon. Among the small number of drug users who had committed a crime with a weapon, 60 percent owned a gun of some kind, whereas only 22 percent of the entire sample owned a gun.

3.   Some changes in these results occur when we include missing cases in the analysis. Relationships between drug sales and possession of a revolver, gun carrying, and firing at someone lose statistical significance for the inmates. For the students, possession of a sawed-off shotgun is not statistically significantly related to drug sales.

6

YOUTH, GANGS, AND GUNS

[W]hen I was first told [by the gang] to shoot somebody . . . I was nervous, but I had this automatic rifle, and when I started to shoot, man, it was easy. . . . [I]t's fast and there's nothing personal in it like when you use a knife.

—Biggy, a Los Angeles Chicano gang member,
quoted by M. S. Jankowski in *Islands in the Street*

Gangs have become the focus of much anticrime attention on the parts of media and government. The seriousness of the gang problem varies across states (California, for example, is considered particularly troubled by gangs) and across cities (large industrial cities like Chicago seem to have the most serious problems). The response to the problem at the local and state levels often is panic (Jackson and Rudman 1993). The federal government too has become preoccupied with gangs recently: in 1992, the FBI made the investigation of street gangs a major law enforcement priority (*New Orleans Times-Picayune* 1992) and the Office of Justice Programs is focusing many of its resources on combatting gangs (Gurule 1991).

Gangs, Weaponry, and Violence

Gangs are thought of popularly as highly involved in firearm use and transport. However, there is surprisingly little available research on the issue of gangs and weapons. Hagedorn (1988:141–43) points to high rates of gun possession among the Milwaukee gang members he studied, and Moore (1991:59–60) attributes rises in violence among Chicano gangs to the increasing presence of guns among gang members. Maxson, Gordon, and Klein (1985; see also Klein, Gordon, and Maxson 1986) report that Los Angeles's gang-related homicides are more likely than non-gang-related homicides to be committed with firearms (see also Spergel 1983; Spergel, Ross, Curry, and Chance 1989). More generally,

95

Jankowski correlates the intensity of gang violence with the availability of weapons to gangs and with their willingness to use them. More sophisticated weaponry "makes it psychologically easy for [gang members] to indulge in such violence" (1991:172). Similarly, Klein and Maxson (1989:219) suggest that, in the gangs' world of confrontational crime and violence, more firearms lead to more attacks, which in turn prompt retaliation. Spergel (1990:190) extends this same theme, noting that more sophisticated weaponry has moved gang violence from foot (i.e., close combat) to vehicle and produced smaller, more mobile attack teams.

Gangs and Violence

Much of the concern about gangs and firearms stems from notions of gang members as particularly criminal and as increasingly involved in drug use and sales—behaviors thought to promote and attract violence. Indeed, gang members apparently are more seriously criminal than are non–gang member offenders (Fagan 1990; Tracy 1987). As well, gangs seem to promote criminality rather than simply to attract more criminal youths (Thornberry et al. 1993). The traditionally best-known gang offense, fighting, is common to most gangs, but seems relatively sporadic, less a goal of the gang than a response to threats to gang solidarity (Spergel 1990; Vigil 1990). To the extent that planned, collective violence characterizes gangs, it occurs to expand gang territories or markets (Jankowski 1991; Padilla 1992).

On the whole, versatility rather than specialization seems the norm regarding such criminal activities as robbery and theft (Klein 1984; Curry and Spergel 1988:382). Gangs whose members are involved in drug use tend to engage in multiple forms of crime (Fagan 1989). Highly organized urban Chinese youth gangs characteristically engage in such diverse activities as street robbery, extortion of businesses, and the gambling rackets (Chin 1990). Chicago Puerto Rican gang members employ numerous methods by which to raise money for their gangs and themselves: burglaries of houses and cars, car thefts, fencing of stolen goods and car parts, dealing drugs (Padilla 1992). Jankowski (1991:132) argues that to the extent that gangs engage collectively in cruder predatory offenses, it is less likely a patterned activity than an ad hoc, emergency measure.

Overall, there is little "conclusive" evidence, according to Spergel (1990:196), of strong links among drug use, drug sales, gang membership, and violence. Regarding drug use and gangs, Fagan (1990) finds a higher prevalence of use among inner-city gang members than among inner-city adolescents in general. Hagedorn (1988) notes widespread drug use among Milwaukee gang members. Moore (1991) reports recent rises in drug use and violence among Los Angeles Chicano gangs. However, in the past, gangs have not engaged heavily in drug use (Spergel 1964; Short and Strodtbeck 1965), and some observers of recent gangs note that while recreational use may be common, addiction is not (Fagan 1989). As noted in the previous chapter, even among gangs engaged in drug sales, drug use may be highly discouraged (Chin 1990; Mieczkowski 1986).

Degree of organization and specialization and their relation to violence are not even wholly clear among gangs whose members *distribute* drugs. In the most specific reference to patterned criminal activity, Skolnick, Bluthenthal, and Correl (1993) argue that Southern California gangs are undergoing a transition from noninstrumental to instrumental organization; the change is shaped by the business nature of the gangs' increased involvement in drug distribution and its equally instrumental attendant violence. Padilla (1992) describes drug selling as the most organized of the many activities engaged in by the Chicago gang members he studied. More cautiously, Fagan (1989, 1990) finds inner-city gang members more heavily involved than non–gang members in drug sales, but he argues also that drug dealing behavior and related organization are highly unevenly distributed across gang types. Important as well, some highly organized and specialized drug distribution organizations term themselves gangs though they possess none of the traditional characteristics of gangs (Mieczkowski 1986; Taylor 1990).

In sum, there is much to learn about gangs and firearms. To the extent that gangs are involved in violence-related activities [and many observers feel they are increasingly so involved (Maxson and Klein 1990; Spergel et al. 1990)], it does seem likely that they acquire and use firearms. But available research does not make even this wholly clear. Our review of the literature regarding gangs and weapons offers little beyond basic observations. We cannot, of course, answer all pertinent questions. But we are able to describe the gun-related activities of the gangs in which our respondents claim membership. We can describe the types of guns these same respondents say they own. We can compare the gun carrying and gun use levels of gang members with those of non–gang members. Finally, we can assess whether or not the type of gang to which the respondent refers (unstructured vs. structured) is linked to firearm-related activity.

Conceptual Issues and Measurement

At the heart of difficulties in describing the gun-related behaviors of gangs are the related problems of conceptualizing "gang" and the link between individual members' and organizations' behaviors. More generally, the extent to which a collection of youths moves from mere group to more formal gang seems positively related to involvement in crime, presumably including gun-related activities (Cartwright, Howard, and Reuterman 1970; Spergel 1990). How patterned are such activities is less well understood. Researchers address the issue differently, depending upon whether their interest is in governance structure or in gang activities. Jankowski (1991), for example, distinguishes three types of gangs according to their authority structures and concludes that the more hierarchically organized a gang, the greater its involvement in collective violence. Fagan (1989), in turn, distinguishes gangs primarily in terms of their involvement in criminal and drug activities. He reports that gangs displaying higher levels of both serious and collective delinquency are more formally structured.

The relation of *individual* gang members' firearm-related activity also is not always clear. On the one hand, there is ample reason to suspect a strong influence of collectivity upon members. Numerous ethnographers and other researchers have argued that gangs (even those of relatively short duration) pursue social solidarity through selective recruitment of youth of like background and maintain it through rites of passage, cultivated loyalty to the gang and its traditions, and subservience to a chain of command (Miller, Geertz, and Cutter 1961; Jansyn 1966; Jackson and McBride 1985; Vigil 1988).

On the other hand, Gottfredson and Hirschi (1990:209) conceptualize gangs as congregations of youths pursuing their individual interests. Klein and Maxson (1989:211) argue that gangs generally are *not* cohesive but instead tend to be more temporary and elastic in structure (and thus in social control efforts). Jankowski (1991) offers a portrait of gangs balancing individual and collective needs: individuals necessarily incorporate into organizations; organizations constantly must accommodate the individual's material and social expectations and sense of autonomy. In short, it is possible that gang and individual gang members' profiles may not be consistent. If gangs are in fact little more than congregations of individuals, there may be no behavioral differences between members of more and of less structured gangs.

Resolution of all of these problems is clearly beyond our present capacity and interest. Nevertheless, awareness of them informed our conceptualization and measurement of gangs. In Chapter 2 we argued that gangs should be defined as such by their members; they should possess, though differentially, such organizational features as a name and designated leadership. Thus, respondents were asked if, in the past year or two (for the inmates, prior to confinement), they belonged to a gang and, if so, whether or not it was organized and possessed a number of characteristics. These included size of the gang and attributes normally associated with gangs: an "official" name, designated leadership, regular meetings, designated clothing, and a specified turf to be defended. "Gangness" was determined by the respondent's designation of his gang as "organized," as opposed to "just a bunch of people." Gang size was collapsed into two categories, one above and the other at or below the mean. A gang attribute score was calculated, and latent class analysis produced a two-class model: structured and unstructured gangs. Two-thirds of our inmate respondents claimed prior affiliation with a gang. Twenty-six percent of the gang members belonged to unstructured gangs and 74 percent to structured gangs. Only 22 percent of the student sample were affiliated with a gang; of those gang members, 57 percent belonged to structured gangs and 43 percent to unstructured gangs.

Our typology admittedly is crude and fails to capture some essential features of gangs, including their differential age structures. Nor can we know whether a respondent's sense of gang attributes and behaviors is influenced by his status within his gang. To the extent this matters, we assume that it is randomly distributed across the sample or addressed through the site control we institute in the multivariate analysis reported at the close of the chapter.

Gangs and Guns

Based on responses to our survey, gangs in fact are highly involved in various forms of gun possession.[1] For the inmates especially, movement from unstructured gang to structured gang brought relatively substantial increases in most of the behaviors in question. More than eight in ten members of structured gangs (85 percent) said that their gang possessed "a stash of guns members can use when they want to" and a nearly equal proportion (88 percent) described guns as plentiful "whenever the gang gets together." Nearly half (46 percent) described gun thefts as a regular gang activity; two-thirds (66 percent) said their gang regularly bought and sold guns. Nine of every ten inmate members of structured gangs (88 percent) stated that most of their gangs' members carried guns. An astonishing 58 percent described "driving around shooting at people you didn't like" as a regular gang activity. For most such behaviors, the percentage of unstructured gang members describing their gangs as participants was smaller than the percentage of structured gang members involved, but nonetheless substantial.[2]

The findings pertaining to the student respondents produced much the same portrait of gangs and guns. Two-thirds (65 percent) of the members of structured gangs described guns as plentiful "whenever the gang got together." Eight in ten (79 percent) said their gang possessed "a stash of guns members could use when they wanted to." A quarter described gun thefts as a regular gang activity; more than four in ten (45 percent) said their gang regularly bought and sold guns. Eight of every ten student members of structured gangs (79 percent) stated that most of their gangs' members carried guns. Twenty-four percent described "driving around shooting at people you didn't like" as a regular gang activity, a percentage much lower than that for inmate structured gangs. As with the inmate respondents, members of unstructured gangs reported lower percentages of gang involvement in these activities than did members of structured gangs.[3]

Individual Gang Members and Guns

As our review of the literature indicated, it is not clear that all gang members behave as their gangs do. In Tables 6.1 and 6.2—for inmate and student respondents, respectively—we examine the gun-related behaviors of individual members of gangs (as opposed to their perceptions of their gangs' activities) as against the same behaviors of non–gang

Table 6.1. Gang Affiliation and Firearm Activity—Inmates[a]

Firearm activity	No gang (%) (N = 338)	Unstructured gang (%) (N = 132)	Structured gang (%) (N = 353)
Possession			
Any type of gun	74	78	93
Revolver	48	55	69
Automatic or semiautomatic handgun	47	51	66
Military-style automatic or semiautomatic rifle	27	24	47
Regular shotgun	30	33	49
Sawed-off shotgun	41	48	61
Owned 3 or more guns	35	44	60
Carrying and use			
Carried gun routinely	44	47	69
Fired at someone	65	67	89

[a] Measurement described in text. Items refer to gun possession immediately prior to confinement. All relationships reported in this table are significant at least at the .05 level.

Table 6.2. Gang Affiliation and Firearm Possession—Students[a]

Firearm possession	No gang (%) (N = 564)	Unstructured gang (%) (N = 99)	Structured gang (%) (N = 65)
Any type of gun	26	58	60
Revolver	11	26	35
Automatic or semiautomatic handgun	13	30	45
Military-style automatic or semiautomatic rifle	4	15	14
Regular shotgun	6	22	28
Sawed-off shotgun	6	16	22
Owned 3 or more guns	6	19	20
Carried gun routinely	9	19	38

[s] Measurement described in text. All relationships reported in this table are significant at least at the .05 level.

members. The comparison also permits examination of differences in levels of involvement in gun-related activities between members of structured and unstructured gangs.

It is apparent from the findings in Table 6.1 that inmate gang members were considerably more involved in firearm activities than were their non–gang counterparts. They were more likely to own every type of gun in question and more likely to carry a gun routinely. Higher percentages of gang members had fired guns at other persons. Table 6.2 indicates much the same findings regarding student gang members.

The same two tables point to differences in level of gun-related activity between members of more and less structured gangs, especially regarding inmates. For all behaviors in question, inmate members of structured gangs were substantially more involved than were their unstructured gang counterparts. Two-thirds of the former owned revolvers and automatic or semiautomatic handguns, for example, while only about half of the latter reported ownership. The percentage of structured gang members who claimed possession of military-style rifles was double that of unstructured gang members. Similar differences characterized routine gun carrying and firing at another person. Overall, the differences between inmate structured and unstructured gang members greatly exceeded those between unstructured gang members and respondents with no gang affiliation (in some instances, the latter two groups differed not at all).

Overall, student members of structured gangs also displayed greater levels of involvement in the behaviors in question than did members of unstructured gangs, and the latter's level of involvement substantially exceeded that of respondents with no gang affiliation. Exceptions pertain to ownership of military-style rifles, of any type of gun generally, and of three or more guns; here gang members exceeded non–gang members in involvement, but degree of gang structure played no role.

Situations of Gun Carrying

In Chapter 4 we explored the various circumstances under which the members of the inmate sample were likely to carry guns; this information was not available for the student sample. In this chapter (Table 6.3), we are able to assess whether or not gang affiliation influences the same behavior though, because we are more interested in gang-related routines, we presently look only at respondents who carried guns "most of the time" or "all of the time" (as opposed to those who carried "never" or "only now and then"). Much as we found in our earlier examination, the likeliest situations of carrying pertained to a sense of the environment as dangerous: respondents carried guns most often when they were in strange areas or out at night or when they perceived themselves as being in need of protection. Overall, however, gang affiliation and degree of gang structure had little influence on these behaviors. Differences pertained to three situations: Members of unstructured gangs were more likely than their two counterparts (who did not differ) to carry a gun during drug deals. Members of structured gangs exceeded their two counterparts (who did not differ) in the likelihood that they would carry guns when out raising hell and when they were in a strange

Table 6.3. Gang Affiliation and Gun-Carrying Situations—Inmates[a]

Very likely to carry a gun when:	No gang (%) (N = 123)	Unstructured gang (%) (N = 53)	Structured gang (%) (N = 233)
Doing a drug deal[b]	71	92	73
Raising hell[b]	48	45	57
In a strange area[b]	81	83	91
At night	83	79	83
Hanging out with friends	53	60	65
Friends were carrying guns	57	57	60
Needing protection	85	82	89
Planning to do a crime	54	52	61

[a] Inmate respondents who had carried guns "now and then" or "most of the time." Measurement described in text.
[b] Significant at the .05 level.

Table 6.4. Gang Affiliation and Gun Dealing—Inmates[a]

Gun dealing	No gang (%) (N = 296)	Unstructured gang (%) (N = 122)	Structured gang (%) (N = 314)
Involved in dealing guns (buying selling, or trading for "a lot of guns"[b]	36	46	68
Gone to places with easy gun laws to buy guns for later sale[b] at least a few times[c]	15	20	29

[a] Measurement described in text.
[b] Significant at .05 level.
[c] "At least a few times" includes "many times," as opposed to "never" and "just once."

area. Regarding the last of these, we assume that members of structured gangs, turf conscious, were more concerned with geographic boundaries and the consequences of crossing them.

Gang Members and Gun Dealing

The common public perception is that gangs "move" a lot of guns: buy, sell, and trade large quantities of guns as their current environments and business interests dictate. In Chapter 3 we examined gun sales for our inmate sample; we lacked comparable data for the student sample. Presently, we can examine the same issue with an eye to differences between gang and non–gang members and between members of structured and unstructured gangs.

As the findings in Table 6.4 indicate, public perceptions are fairly accurate regarding gangs and gun sales. Gang members were more likely than non–gang members to identify themselves as having dealt guns and as having bought guns in places with more lenient laws for the purpose of selling them at a later date. Clearly, degree of structure of the respondent's gang influenced his answers to these items. Members of structured gangs were about 50 percent more likely to engage in gun sales than were members of unstructured gangs.

Gangs and Motivations for Firearm Activity

If gang members are more involved in gun-related activities and structured gangs are more involved than are unstructured gangs in those same activities, what accounts for it? Is there something about the gang per se that perpetuates gun behaviors? Is gun carrying, for example, intrinsically valued by gang members? Or are gang members more involved in firearm-related activities because more of their members engage in behaviors that "require" guns—crime and drug distribution, for instance? In this section, we explore such possibilities.

Status Enhancement, Gangs, and Guns

We reported in Chapter 4 that status enhancement played little role in the decision of either inmate or student to arm himself. Nonetheless, some respondents did agree that respect from their peers derived in part from gun ownership and that their friends would look down upon them if they did not carry a gun. Given the apparent strength of the social bond among members of gangs, we would expect that status enhancement would be likely to play a role in gun possession. In fact, while the

Table 6.5. Gang Affiliation, Status Enhancement, and Firearm Activity—Inmates[a]

	Agree that peer respect follows gun possession[b]		
	No gang (%) (N = 279)	Unstructured gang (%) (N = 118)	Structured gang (%) (N = 328)
Firearm activity	No/yes	No/yes	No/yes
Possession			
Any type of gun	73/86	77/92	94/90
Revolver	47/50	54/77	70/67
Automatic or semiautomatic handgun	47/50	51/54	67/62
Military-style automatic or semiautomatic rifle	24/42*	23/23	46/48
Regular shotgun	29/31	35/33	46/50
Sawed-off shotgun	39/47	47/54	56/62
Owned 3 or more guns	30/40	42/45	56/62
Carrying and use			
Carried gun routinely	39/69*	45/68	69/71
Fired at someone	61/86*	67/69	91/78*

[a] Measurement described in text. Items refer to gun possession immediately prior to confinement.
[b] Item: "In my crowd, if you don't have a gun, people don't respect you."
* Significant at least at .05 level.

Table 6.6. Gang Affiliation, Status Enhancement, and Firearm Possession—
   Students[a]

	Agree that peer respect follows gun possession[b]		
	No gang (%) (N = 445)	Unstructured gang (%) (N = 77)	Structured gang (%) (N = 46)
Firearm possession	No/yes	No/yes	No/yes
Any type of gun	79/69	51/80	57/82
Revolver	9/18	24/40	29/64
Automatic or semiautomatic handgun	10/15	29/30	43/46
Military-style automatic or semiautomatic rifle	3/5	12/20	11/36
Regular shotgun	5/6	6/34*	26/30
Sawed-off shotgun	3/8	9/50*	17/46
Owned 3 or more guns	3/5	13/24	21/26
Carried gun routinely	6/15*	17/30	29/55

[a] Measurement described in text.
[b] Item: "In my crowd, if you don't have a gun, people don't respect you."
* Significant at least at .05 level.

vast majority of non–gang and gang members of both our samples did not view gun possession as a component of status enhancement, gang membership did influence the relationship for students though not for inmates. Among the student respondents, agreement that peers do not respect those who do not possess a gun and agreement that one's friends would look negatively upon one for failing to carry a gun were positively, if weakly related to gang membership and, for gang members, to affiliation with a structured rather than an unstructured gang.[4]

Whether or not any such relationship translates into involvement in various kinds of firearm-related activities can be ascertained through examination of Tables 6.5 and 6.6. The tables display the relationship between status enhancement and gun possession, carrying, and (for inmates) use for respondents who were not affiliated with a gang and for members of both unstructured and structured gangs. It is clear that, for both inmate and student samples, there was little relationship between status enhancement and gun-related activity for either gang or non–gang respondents. The social bonding that apparently occurs among gang members did not result in social pressure to bear arms among our respondents.

Violent Crime, Gangs, and Guns

A link between violent criminality and gang membership also is a relative staple of media discussions of urban youth and social problems; this seems particularly true of entertainment media. Our data suggest that the media are accurate in their portrayal. For both our samples, involvement in violent crime (armed robbery for inmates; crimes committed with weapons for students) was higher for gang than for non–gang members and was less in evidence for unstructured than for structured gang members.[5] Again, what is of interest presently is whether or not, within and without gangs, violent criminality is related to involvement in firearm-related activities. To this end, Tables 6.7 and 6.8 display the relationship between commission of violent offenses and gun possession, carrying, and (for inmates) use for respondents who were not affiliated with a gang and for members of both unstructured and structured gangs.

The findings displayed in both tables mirror those reported in Chapter 4: involvement in violent crime was related to most forms of gun possession, carrying, and use for both samples. The same findings make

Table 6.7.   Gang Affiliation, Violent Crime, and Firearm Activity—Inmates[a]

	Committed armed robbery		
Firearm activity	No gang (%) (N = 338) No/yes	Unstructured gang (%) (N = 132) No/yes	Structured gang (%) (N = 353) No/yes
Possession			
Any type of gun	65/88*	69/90*	87/97*
Revolver	41/57*	42/72*	64/72
Automatic or semiautomatic handgun	38/57*	42/62*	55/73*
Military-style automatic or semiautomatic rifle	24/32	20/29	45/48
Regular shotgun	26/36	28/40	42/53*
Sawed-off shotgun	30/57*	37/62*	51/67*
Owned 3 or more guns	28/46*	34/57*	50/66*
Carrying and use			
Carried gun routinely	36/56*	38/59*	57/77*
Fired at someone	55/80*	57/80*	78/96*

[s] Measurement described in text. Items refer to gun possession immediately prior to confinement.
* Significant at least at .05 level.

Table 6.8. Gang Affiliation, Violent Crime, and Firearm Possession—Students[a]

| | Committed crime with weapon | | |
	No gang (%) (N = 541) No/yes	Unstructured gang (%) (N = 94) No/yes	Structured gang (%) (N = 60) No/yes
Firearm possession			
Any type of gun	22/46*	52/85*	52/87*
Revolver	10/15	20/54*	30/56
Automatic or semiautomatic handgun	10/24*	26/31	41/56
Military-style automatic or semiautomatic rifle	3/6	14/31	7/31
Regular shotgun	4/21*	16/54*	23/43
Sawed-off shotgun	4/18*	16/54*	14/44*
Owned 3 or more guns	3/18*	11/54*	14/38*
Carried gun routinely	6/15	10/53*	26/75*

[a] Measurement described in text.
* Significant at least at .05 level.

clear as well that gang membership had little bearing on this relationship. That is, among inmate respondents, armed robbery and gun possession, carrying, and use went hand in hand for non–gang members and gang members alike and for members of unstructured as well as structured gangs. Among student respondents, commission of crimes with weapons was related to gun possession and carrying no matter the status of gang affiliation. Ultimately, then, it may not be gang membership—generally or with respect to type of gang—that increases the chances of gun-related activity. It may be, instead, that gangs attract more violent offenders and, therefore, more firearm activity.

Drug Activity, Gangs, and Guns

Drug use and distribution are not uncommon but also are by no means universal gang activities. Our own data regarding hard-drug use and gang membership indicate that, among inmates, use is unrelated to gang membership and, among gang members, to gang structure. Among students, gang members reported significantly higher levels of drug use than did non–gang members though structure of the gang had no influence on drug use.[6] The findings regarding drug distribution indicate that, among respondents of both samples, drug selling was higher among gang members but that members of unstructured and structured gangs did not differ in involvement in sales.[7] As we have

done with the other potential motivations to engage in gun-related behavior among gang members, we examine in Tables 6.9 through 6.12, for
inmates and students respectively, the relationship between drug use
and distribution and gun possession, carrying, and (for inmates) use for
respondents who were not affiliated with a gang and for members of
both unstructured and structured gangs.

As was indicated in Chapter 5, hard-drug use was not linked to
firearm-related activity. This finding appears again in Tables 6.9 and
6.10. With only a few exceptions, drug use was not predictive of firearm
possession, carrying, and use for members of either sample and across
all three categories of gang affiliation. As the findings presented in Tables 6.11 and 6.12 indicate, drug selling did predict these behaviors for
both samples—as it did more generally in Chapter 5. However, among
inmates, the relationship held for non–gang members and members of
unstructured gangs relatively evenly; it was considerably less obvious
among members of structured gangs. For student respondents, drug
selling was clearly linked to gun possession and carrying among non–
gang members but, with two exceptions (possession of an automatic or
semiautomatic handgun and routine gun carrying by members of un-

Table 6.9. Gang Affiliation, Hard Drug Use, and Firearm Activity—Inmates[a]

	Used hard drugs		
Firearm activity	No gang (%) (N = 272) No/yes	Unstructured gang (%) (N = 118) No/yes	Structured gang (%) (N = 291) No/yes
Possession			
Any type of gun	68/79*	75/79	91/95
Revolver	44/49	60/53	72/66
Automatic or semiautomatic handgun	44/44	48/53	64/65
Military-style automatic or semiautomatic rifle	26/27	31/15	47/45
Regular shotgun	24/33	34/36	40/55*
Sawed-off shotgun	39/40	45/57	54/64
Owned 3 or more guns	33/33	42/47	56/61
Carrying and Use			
Carried gun routinely	37/40	45/49	69/68
Fired at someone	60/66	63/70	90/88

[a] Measurement described in text. Items refer to gun possession immediately
prior to confinement.
* Significant at least at .05 level.

Table 6.10. Hard Drug Use, Gang Affiliation, and Firearm Possession—Students[a]

	Used Hard Drugs		
	No gang (%) (N = 565)	Unstructured gang (%) (N = 98)	Structured gang (%) (N = 65)
Firearm possession	No/yes	No/yes	No/yes
Any type of gun	26/31	57/58	58/70
Revolver	11/13	26/25	35/40
Automatic or semiautomatic handgun	13/13	29/33	46/40
Military-style automatic or semiautomatic rifle	4/0	16/8	13/20
Regular shotgun	6/13	21/33	26/40
Sawed-off shotgun	5/19	15/25	22/20
Owned 3 or more guns	5/6	19/25	20/20
Carried gun routinely	8/17	15/54*	38/40

[a] Measurement described in text.
* Significant at least at .05 level.

Table 6.11. Gang Affiliation, Drug Sales, and Firearm Activity—Inmates[a]

	Sold drugs		
	No gang (%) (N = 337)	Unstructured gang (%) (N = 132)	Structured gang (%) (N = 350)
Firearm activity	No/yes	No/yes	No/yes
Possession			
Any type of gun	66/82*	60/88*	87/96
Revolver	42/53*	36/66*	65/71
Automatic or semiautomatic handgun	35/56*	34/60*	57/70*
Military-style automatic or semiautomatic rifle	21/33*	13/31*	46/47
Regular shotgun	26/35	28/37	49/48
Sawed-off shotgun	33/49	30/58*	51/66*
Owned 3 or more guns	27/43*	30/52*	53/63
Carrying and use			
Carried gun routinely	35/52*	38/52	61/74*
Fired at someone	55/74*	50/77*	84/92

[a] Measurement described in text. Items refer to gun possession immediately prior to confinement.
* Significant at least at .05 level.

Table 6.12. Gang Affiliation, Drug Sales, and Firearm Possession—Students[a]

	Sold Drugs		
Firearm possession	No gang (%) (N = 565) No/yes	Unstructured gang (%) (N = 98) No/yes	Structured gang (%) (N = 65) No/yes
Any type of gun	22/58*	52/71	57/67
Revolver	8/32*	23/32	34/39
Automatic or semiautomatic handgun	10/37*	21/50*	38/61
Military-style automatic or semiautomatic rifle	3/7	14/18	13/17
Regular shotgun	5/16*	21/25	32/17
Sawed-off shotgun	5/11	16/18	19/28
Owned 3 or more guns	5/12*	17/25	19/22
Carried gun routinely	6/25*	14/32*	36/44

[a] Measurement described in text.
* Significant at least at .05 level.

structured gangs) was decidedly unrelated to these behaviors among gang members. In short, involvement in drug distribution may account for the higher involvement of non–gang members and of members of unstructured gangs in *some* forms of gun-related behavior. Overall, involvement in drug distribution does not appear to account for the higher levels of firearm-related activity by members of structured gangs.

Exposure to Gun Threats, Gangs, and Guns

We turn now to a potentially key element of life in a gang: risk of becoming a gunshot victim. Are gang members more likely to carry guns because they occupy especially dangerous niches within their social worlds? Asked otherwise, do gang members carry guns because they perceive others to be gunning for them? In seeking an answer, we employ the same measure of such risk that we have in the logistic regression analyses reported in previous chapters. Respondents in both samples were asked whether or not they personally had been threatened with a gun or shot at. Presently, we distinguish between those who have been threatened or shot at a few or many times from those who have never or only once experienced such an event.[8]

Importantly, we do not assume here that this measure taps victimization, for it is quite possible that respondents had been fired upon by persons against whom they were committing crimes, by participants in drug deals gone sour, or by other persons against whom respondents were directing aggression. Nor do we assume that gun possession followed threat. It is equally likely that gun possession placed respondents in situations of threat. Our intent is simply to measure the extent to which a respondent exists in a hostile environment and thus runs the risk of harm.

Our data suggest that gang membership does increase the likelihood of being threatened with a gun or shot at. For the inmate respondents, members of structured gangs were 40 percent more likely than members of unstructured gangs to have experienced such an event. However, members of unstructured gangs were only 6 percent more likely to have been so threatened than were those not affiliated with gangs. For the student respondents, the pattern was more dramatic. Those who belonged to structured gangs were 44 percent more likely to have been threatened or shot at with a gun than were members of unstructured gangs. The latter, in turn, were more than twice as likely to have experienced such an event.[9]

Does the relationship between gang membership and exposure to gun

Table 6.13. Gang Affiliation, Prior Gun Threats, and Firearm Activity—Inmates[a]

	Exposure to gun threats[b]		
	No gang (%) (N = 337)	Unstructured gang (%) (N = 132)	Structured gang (%) (N = 350)
Firearm activity	No/yes	No/yes	No/yes
Possession			
Any type of gun	58/91*	60/95*	83/96*
Revolver	35/61*	31/74*	58/72*
Automatic or semiautomatic handgun	33/59*	29/68*	51/70*
Military-style automatic or semiautomatic rifle	17/37*	15/31*	30/52*
Regular shotgun	28/57*	32/55*	32/52*
Sawed-off shotgun	29/53*	28/63*	51/63*
Owned 3 or more guns	24/46*	26/58*	46/64*
Carrying and use			
Carried gun routinely	28/59*	26/62*	49/75*
Fired at someone	48/81*	40/87*	69/95*

[a] Measurement described in text. Items refer to gun possession immediately prior to confinement.
[b] Respondent has personally been threatened with a gun or shot at a few or many times (as opposed to never or once).
* Significant at least at .05 level.

Table 6.14. Gang Affiliation, Prior Gun Threats, and Firearm Possession—Students[a]

	Exposure to gun threats[b]		
Firearm possession	No gang (%) (N = 565) No/yes	Unstructured gang (%) (N = 98) No/yes	Structured gang (%) (N = 65) No/yes
Any type of gun	24/40*	52/68	55/67
Revolver	9/19*	19/38*	21/50*
Automatic or semiautomatic handgun	12/20*	25/38	42/47
Military-style automatic or semiautomatic rifle	4/3	14/18	6/22
Regular shotgun	5/6	13/19	13/28
Sawed-off shotgun	5/9	16/18	12/31
Owned 3 or more guns	18/36*	41/56	46/66
Carried gun routinely	7/13	15/26	19/56*

[a] Measurement described in text.
[b] Respondent has personally been threatened with a gun or shot at a few or many times (as opposed to never or once).
* Significant at least at .05 level.

threats bear on differential involvement in firearm-related activity across gang and non–gang members? The answer regarding the inmate respondents is decidedly yes. As the findings in Table 6.13 indicate, prior gun threats were significantly related to every form of gun possession, carrying, and use examined among each type of gang category examined. Among student respondents, the relationship is less obvious. As indicated in Table 6.14, ownership of a revolver was tied to prior gun threats for non–gang respondents and for both types of gang members. Non–gang respondents who had been threatened were also more likely to have owned an automatic or semiautomatic handgun and, more generally, to have owned any type of gun or three or more guns. Beyond this, gang membership counts for nothing in the present context except, importantly, that members of structured gangs who had been threatened or shot at were more likely than those who had not to have carried a gun routinely. This was not the case for members of the two comparison groups.

In sum, while we are uncertain whether or not occupation of a hostile environment is essential to explaining a student gang member's greater involvement in firearm-related behaviors, we note with certainty that hostile environment does account for at least some of the difference in possession, carrying, and use of firearms between those inmates who were affiliated with structured gangs and those who were either affiliated with unstructured gangs or with no gang. Hostile environment also appears to explain differences between unstructured and structured gang members in these same behaviors.

Multivariate Considerations

We recognize that many of the variables we have examined as potentially influencing gun-related behavior may be strongly related to each other; gang membership is no exception. The logistic regression results presented in Tables 6.15 (inmates) and 6.16 (students) reflect our attempt

Table 6.15. Logistic Regression of Firearm-Related Activities on Motivational, Drug and Gang Activity, Sociodemographic, and Site Variables—Inmate Sample (N = 530)

	Beta coefficients				
	Owned handgun		Owned sawed-off shotgun	Carried gun routinely	Fired gun at someone
Variable	Auto/ semiauto	Revolver			
Criminal activity	.224*	.203*	.277*	.278*	.401*
Status enhancement	−.044	−.113	.067	.105	−.081
Prior gun threats	.760*	.621*	.513*	.987*	1.104*
Drug use	−.012	−.103*	−.035	.016	−.058
Drug sales	.531*	.420	.871*	.550*	.637*
Gang member[a]					
Unstructured gang	−.269	.143	.263	−.133	−.274
Structured gang	.117	.348	.176	.474	.497
Age	.030	.012	.022	−.087	−.008
Race/Ethnicity[b]					
Black	−.058	−.359	−.377	.126	.377
Hispanic	−.153	−.114	−.083	−.125	.243
White	−.093	−.307	−.453	−.287	.042
City size	.012	.015	−.047	.001	.031
Site[c]					
California	−.010	.677*	.392	.604	.659
Illinois	−.619	.759	.384	.626	.781
Louisiana	.555	1.058*	.671	.461	.262
Constant	−2.173	−1.706	−2.459	−1.721	−2.181
Model χ^2 (df = 15)	118.321*	101.523*	112.479*	178.264*	182.442*

* $p < .05$.
[a] Non-gang member omitted.
[b] "Other" omitted.
[c] New Jersey omitted.

Table 6.16. Logistic Regression of Firearm-Related Activities on Motivational, Drug and Gang Activity, Sociodemographic, and Site Variables—Student Sample ($N = 465$)

	Beta coefficients			
	Owned handgun		Owned	Carried gun
Variable	Auto/semiauto	Revolver	sawed-off shotgun	routinely
Criminal activity	.456	−.132	1.379*	1.637*
Status enhancement	.053	.289	.274	.004
Prior gun threats	.456*	.516*	−.217	.267
Drug use	−.034	−.005	.062	−.001
Drug sales	1.783*	.958*	1.136*	1.666*
Gang member[a]				
Unstructured gang	.344	.383	.331	−.086
Structured gang	1.003*	.478	1.264*	.687
Age	.126	.027	.273	.116
Race/ethnicity[b]				
Black	.217	.121	−.292	.858
Hispanic	−.494	−.447	−1.757	.110
Site[c]				
California	.927	.468	7.658	1.793*
Illinois	1.118*	.701	7.658	.617
Louisiana	.742	.083	6.742	1.375*
Constant	−5.868	−3.942	−15.339	−7.104
Model χ^2 (df = 13)	100.070*	55.559*	51.612*	75.335*

* $p < .05$.
[s] Non-gang member omitted.
[b] "Other" omitted.
[c] New Jersey omitted.

to address this possibility. Importantly, while the inclusion and exclusion of missing cases had little effect on multivariate outcomes in prior chapters, they are more telling here.

Excluding missing cases, as has been our practice throughout this study, we find our regression results essentially confirming those reported throughout this chapter. At least among our inmate respondents, once the effects of involvement in criminal and drug activity and prior gun threats were controlled, gang membership had little effect on the possession, carrying, and use of firearms. Among the student respondents, the picture differed somewhat. Members of structured gangs were more likely to possess automatic or semiautomatic handguns and sawed-off shotguns than were non–gang members and members of unstructured gangs (who did not differ in involvement in these behaviors). Yet, these findings are muddied somewhat when we introduce the missing cases into the analysis. For the inmate sample, structured gang membership attained statistically significant relationships with all but possession of a sawed-off shotgun, though the findings regarding unstructured gang membership remained the same.[10] Among student respondents, membership in a structured gang became significantly statistically related to all four gun-related behaviors. With one exception (possession of an automatic or semiautomatic handgun), unstructured gang membership remained unrelated to the behaviors in question.[11]

In short, it may well be that aspects of membership in a structured gang do account for higher levels of firearm-related behavior apart from the influential effects of other independent variables. The possibility awaits further research. Beyond this, however, it is noteworthy that the same variables appear in the present analysis to influence gun-related behavior as have consistently done so in prior chapters (this time net of the effects of gang membership): criminal activity, prior gun threats, and drug distribution.

Summary

Are gangs at the heart of America's problem of youths and guns? Our findings point to a definite relationship, though they also suggest that it is far from a simple one. To the extent that we may generalize from our present findings, gangs engage in high levels of firearm possession, carrying, and use—at least as their individual members describe them. Individual gang members participate in firearm-related activity to a greater extent than do individuals who are not affiliated with gangs. To the extent that the gang to which an individual belongs is structured (a more formal, classic-style gang), involvement in these activities increases.

Why these findings are so is less clear. Is there something about gangs per se that accounts for them or do gangs simply engage in more of the behaviors commonly associated with gun possession and use? It appears from our findings that the need for status enhancement—thought commonsensically so important among gang members—does not account for higher levels of gun use among gang members. Violent criminality is related to firearm-related activity, but our findings suggest that the relationship holds across non–gang and gang categories. Indeed, violent criminality seems more characteristic of non–gang individuals than of gang members and less common among structured than among unstructured gang members. Drug use seems no more frequent among gang members than among youth unaffiliated with gangs (though, among our student respondents, some evidence of a connection existed), and our findings do not point to it as related to firearm activity differentials. Drug sales seem more common among gang members than among those without gang member status but not more common among structured as opposed to unstructured gang members. Yet, here again, the relationship between gun-related behaviors and drug sales seems strongest for non–gang members and weakest (though clearly at work) among members of structured gangs.

We suspect that what lies behind at least a portion of the differential involvement in firearm-related activity by gang members is the degree to which they live in a dangerous social world. This clearly is the case among youths like those in our inmate sample. It seems to us that, overall, gang members are more visible in a hostile world than are youths who do not belong to gangs. They are more turf conscious. They cluster. They wear apparel that signals solidarity and aggression. They are targets of violence by virtue of their aggression against other gangs and their efforts to avoid counteraggression.

We have no data bearing directly on this conclusion, but we do note that, among our inmate respondents—gang and non–gang members alike—the perceived need for protection and the traversing of strange areas highly influenced gun-carrying behavior. As well, prior exposure to threats of gun violence (whether or not accumulated in socially acceptable roles) was a clear predictor of most forms of gun possession, carrying, and use among our respondents. Among the inmate respondents, structured gang members reported significantly higher levels of such exposure, and exposure predicted gun-related activity within this subset.

Our attempt to sort out these issues through multivariate analysis has been compromised somewhat by the problem of differential impact of missing cases. To the extent that gang membership bears on gun possession, carrying, and use independent of drug distribution profile and prior exposure to gun threats (as well as the other variables of interest in this study), it seems to more likely to do so among members of structured gangs.

Ultimately, of course, we must offer the same caveat about gangs and guns as we did about drugs and guns. There is a considerable difference between pointing to a relationship and arguing that it causes all our troubles. Gang members may engage to greater degrees in gun activity, but our findings point unequivocally to high levels of gun possession, carrying, and use among adolescents who are not affiliated with gangs. We have found no magical, single-variable, explanatory bullet—no "single-variable" answer—in this chapter nor, more generally, in this study. In other words, like drugs, gangs may well be a part of the answer to the "kids and violence" question, but the high level of possession and carrying among non–gang teens implies that we would continue to have a problem with juveniles and firearms even if every gang in every city disappeared tomorrow.

Notes

1.   A number of items were presented to respondents of both samples who reported belonging to gangs. One set was introduced this way: "Was your gang or group ever involved with any of the following activities? Stealing guns. Buying and selling guns. Shooting guns. Driving around shooting at people you didn't like." For each activity item, three responses were possible: "yes, regularly," "yes, from time to time," "never." A second set was introduced this way: "Following are some statements that may or may not be true of your gang or group. For each statement, indicate whether that is true or not of your gang or group: 'Most of the people in my gang or group carry guns'. 'There are always lots of guns around whenever the gang or group get together'. 'You have to have a gun to join my gang or group'. 'You have to show you can use a gun to be in my gang or group.' 'My gang or group has a stash of guns members can use when they want to.'" Statements were phrased in the past tense for inmate respondents. For each item, respondents could indicate "yes" or "no."

2.   Six in ten members of structured gangs (58 percent) reported that their gang possessed "a stash of guns members can use when they want to," and 60 percent) described guns as plentiful "whenever the gang gets together." Nearly a quarter (23 percent) described gun thefts as a regular gang activity; one-third (35 percent) reported that their gang regularly bought and sold guns. Sixty-two percent stated that most of their gangs' members carried guns. One-third (34 percent) described "driving around shooting at people you didn't like" as a regular gang activity.

3.   One-third (35 percent) described guns as plentiful "whenever the gang gets together," and 49 percent said their gang possessed "a stash of guns members can use when they want to." One in ten (11 percent) described gun thefts as a regular gang activity; 19 percent said that their gang regularly bought and sold guns. Four of every ten (42 percent) stated that most of their gangs' members carried guns. Fifteen percent described "driving around shooting at people you didn't like" as a regular gang activity.

4.   Specifically, 24 percent of the student structured gang members agreed that peers do not respect those who do not possess a gun; only 13

percent of members of unstructured gangs and 9 percent of those un-affiliated with a gang agreed (p = .028). While 22 percent of those affili-ated with structured gangs agreed that one's friends would look down on one for failing to carry a gun, only 10 percent of those in unstructured gangs and 7 percent of those who did not belong to a gang agreed (p = .049).

5.   Sixty-one percent of the inmate members of structured gangs had committed armed robbery; 42 percent of unstructured gang mem-bers and 38 percent of unaffiliated respondents had committed that crime (p = .000). Among students, 27 percent who claimed structured gang affiliation had committed a crime with a weapon, while only 16 percent of the members of unstructured gangs and 7 percent of those who were not affiliated with gangs had committed such a crime (p = .000).

6.   Fifteen percent of structured gang members reported hard-drug use; 12 percent of unstructured gang members reported hard-drug use; and only 3 percent of those who did not belong to gangs had used hard drugs.

7.   Among inmate respondents, 66 percent of the members of struc-tured gangs and 64 percent of those in unstructured gangs had sold drugs; 51 percent of those unaffiliated with gangs had done so (p = .000). Among student respondents, 28 percent of both structured and unstructured gang members had sold drugs, but only 10 percent of non–gang members had done so (p = .000).

8.   Since the item contained no temporal element, the categoriza-tion system was thought to increase the likelihood that the threat events were more recent.

9.   Among inmate respondents, 78 percent of those in structured gangs, 56 percent of those in unstructured gangs, and 50 percent of those unaffiliated with gangs had been shot at or threatened with a gun. Within the student sample, 49 percent of the structured gang members, 34 percent of the unstructured gang members, and 14 percent of those who did not belong to a gang had been threatened or shot at with a gun.

10.   When missing cases were included in the analysis, drug use also was no longer significantly related to possession of a revolver and drug sales were no longer significantly related to the routine carrying of a firearm and to having fired a gun at someone.

11.   Here, the inclusion of missing cases resulted in a lack of statisti-cal significance regarding the link between prior gun threats and posses-sion of an automatic or semi-automatic handgun; it also resulted in the presence of a significant relationship between gun threats and routine gun carrying. Drug dealing no longer was related to possession of a sawed-off shotgun.

7

RELATED THEMES FOR RESEARCH

> Danny [a New Orleans suburban teenager, sixteen,] was 11 when he got his first handgun. . . . Since then, he has illegally purchased several other handguns and now shares a .22-caliber sawed-off rifle with some friends. . . . Carl, 19, of [a New Orleans suburb] . . . has been shot nine times in two separate incidents. . . . Said one boy from a middle-class neighborhood: "It's straight-up dangerous out there."
>
> —"Kids and Guns," *New Orleans Times-Picayune*

Our focus to this point has been on the same segment of the population that captures the attention of legislators, law enforcement personnel, and the media: inner-city, adolescent males. We have described the guns they acquire, why they carry guns, how they use firearms, their connections to the worlds of drugs and gangs. But there are other questions to be asked about kids and guns, questions that ultimately deserve the same degree of scrutiny that we have given our present topic and sample. In this chapter, we will explore briefly three such questions. First, what of inner-city females? They live in the same dangerous environments as do the males we have studied here. Do they acquire and carry firearms at comparable rates? Second, who are the victims of adolescents' use of firearms: innocent bystanders or juveniles involved more proactively in the cycle of violence? Finally, what of the suburbs: are guns in the hands of adolescents a problem there too?

Girls and Guns[1]

Few people think of female adolescents when they consider the problem of guns in this society, but the pattern of criminal activities by females, save for the most serious of violent offenses, greatly resembles that of young male offenders (Steffensmeier and Allan 1995). Given these similarities, there is no reason to *assume* that females are uninvolved in firearm-related activity.

119

There is little by way of a research literature against which to test this assumption. Sixteen percent of female adolescents in select urban neighborhoods reported having carried unspecified weapons illegally in the course of the year prior to being surveyed (Fagan 1990). A 1990 survey of 11,631 students in grades nine through twelve found that 8 percent of the female respondents had carried a weapon to school; the weapon may or may not have been a firearm (U.S. Department of Health and Human Services 1991). Seven percent of the females in a sample of public high school students in a midwestern city had carried an unspecified weapon to school at least once over the course of a year (Asmussen 1992). In fact, only two studies refer directly to firearms: (a) Sadowski et al. (1989) found that 1 percent of a 1987 nonurban sample of female adolescents owned a handgun; and (b) slightly more than 1 percent of the females in a 1990 sample of Seattle eleventh-grade students reported owning a handgun (Callahan and Rivara 1992). In short, we have only the most general information about female firearm activities. Some studies fail to specify the type of weapon in question; most do not delve into patterns of firearm acquisition and carrying.

As we noted at the beginning of this book, we collected data from inner-city females as well as from males. Relative to the involvement of high school boys in gun-related behaviors, high school girls' involvement was sufficiently low that we chose to address it separately. The patterns nonetheless are intriguing.

Exposure to Firearms

As they were for the males in our sample, firearms were characteristic of the immediate social environments of the female respondents. As indicated in Table 7.1, a substantial majority (68 percent) of respondents reported that males in their families owned guns; half of these indicated that most or all of their male relatives did so. Forty-two percent reported that these same males carried guns outside the home routinely. A third of the respondents reported that their friends owned guns; a slightly smaller percentage (28) indicated that these friends carried their guns outside the home regularly. Forty-five percent noted that they knew of at least one person who had carried a gun to school within the past year; 5 percent indicated that they knew of many persons who had done so.

Many of the respondents had been exposed in some fashion to gun-related violence. Thirteen percent reported that they had been threatened with a gun "in the last few years" while traveling to and from school. Six percent reported having been shot at on at least one occasion. The respondents reported that classmates also had a high level of victimization experiences involving guns. For instance, 43 percent indi-

Table 7.1. Female Respondents' Exposure to Firearms

Items	(N)	%
Guns among family and friends		
Males in the family owning guns	(790)	
None		32
Some of them		38
Most of them		20
All of them		10
Males in the family routinely carrying guns outside their homes	(790)	
None		58
Some of them		28
Most of them		9
All of them		5
Friends owning guns	(784)	
None		67
Some of them		24
Most of them		7
All of them		2
Friends routinely carrying guns outside the home	(783)	
None		72
Some of them		19
Most of them		7
All of them		2
Personally knows someone who has carried a gun to school in the past year	(804)	
No		55
Yes, just one		18
Yes, a few		21
Yes, many		6
Exposure to firearm violence		
While in school or on the way to and from school in the last few years, has respondent:		
Been threatened with a gun	(733)	
Never		87
Once		8
A few times		4
Many times		1
Been shot at with a gun	(733)	
Never		94
Once		4
A few times		1
Many times		1

continued

Table 7.1.   Continued

Items	(N)	%
In the last few years, have any students respondent knows personally in school:		
Been threatened with a gun	(719)	
None		57
One or two		24
A few		13
Many		6
Been shot at with a gun	(714)	
None		55
One or two		20
Yes, a few		14
Many		10

cated that they knew someone personally who had been threatened with a gun; 44 percent knew of someone who had been shot at.

Gun Possession and Carrying

As indicated in Table 7.2, 9 percent of the sample reported having owned a revolver in the course of their lives, 5 percent had owned an automatic or semiautomatic handgun, regular shotguns were owned by 7 percent of the respondents, and other types of firearms were owned by fewer than 5 percent of the sample. Among guns *currently* in the students' possession, revolvers were again most likely to be owned (6 percent). Shotguns and automatic or semiautomatic handguns were the next most popular: 4 percent of the sample reported that they owned one or the other.

As we noted for male respondents, gun ownership does not equate necessarily with the carrying of guns outside the home. Responses to items concerning gun carrying also are shown in Table 7.2. While 89 percent of the sample reported that they never carried firearms, 11 percent indicated that they carried a gun at least "now and then," though only 1 percent did so "all the time." Only 3 percent of the students reported carrying a gun to school on some occasion, with less than 1 percent claiming to do so "all the time."

Motives for Gun Carrying

We noted that a perceived need for protection seemed to motivate gun acquisition and carrying among the male inner-city students we studied. We find an even more pronounced pattern of protection-oriented behavior among our female respondents. Shown in Table 7.3 are responses from those who reported possessing a handgun (the most commonly owned gun); they refer to the respondent's "most recent handgun." By far the major reason cited for obtaining such a weapon was self-protection. Virtually all of those possessing a handgun cited this factor, 89 percent deeming it "very important." Presumably in the same vein, 52 percent felt it was important to be armed because they believed their enemies had guns. Beyond this, a host of other reasons were reported, though they assumed considerably less importance. Roughly 27 percent reported that they wanted a handgun "to get some-

Table 7.2. Female Respondents' Gun Ownership and Carrying

Item	(N)	%
Lifetime ownership[a]		
Hunting rifle	(824)	3
Regular shotgun	(823)	7
Sawed-off shotgun	(823)	3
Military-style rifle	(822)	3
Revolver	(891)	9
Automatic or semiautomatic handgun	(819)	5
Current ownership[b]		
Hunting rifle	(814)	2
Regular shotgun	(812)	4
Sawed-off shotgun	(814)	2
Military-style rifle	(814)	1
Revolver	(813)	6
Automatic or semiautomatic handgun	(813)	4
Respondent carries a gun outside the home but not at school, including in car	(762)	
All the time		1
Most of the time		2
Only now and then		8
Never		89
Respondent carries gun when at school	(775)	
All the time		<1
Most of the time		1
Only now and then		2
Never		97

[a] Item: "For every weapon on the list, please indicate whether you personally have ever owned such a weapon, or had such a weapon that you considered yours even if you did not actually own it."
[b] Item: "Which of the following kinds of guns do you own or possess at this time?"

Table 7.3. Reasons for Obtaining Most Recent Handgun and Source of Gun—
Female Respondents Claiming to Have Obtained a Handgun

		How important?		
Reason[a]	*(N)*	*Very (%)*	*Somewhat (%)*	*Not (%)*
To protect myself	(71)	89	10	1
All my enemies were carrying guns	(56)	27	25	48
Needed a gun to get somebody	(56)	9	18	73
To impress people	(56)	7	2	91
All my friends were carrying guns	(56)	4	13	83
To sell	(54)	2	7	91

Source[b] (N = 74)	%
From a friend	41
From a member of my family	30
From a gun shop	9
Off the street	8
From a drug dealer or addict	8
All other	4

[a] Item: "Look over the list below and circle [the response] which comes closest to saying how *important* that reason was to you when you obtained your most recent handgun."
[b] Item: "Please circle below the [means] that best says *where* you got your most recent handgun."

one," though only 9 percent said this was "very important." Even fewer said they obtained handguns because their friends had them, to impress people, or to sell.

Acquisition of Firearms

Table 7.3 also explores the issue of the means by which our respondents reported obtaining their firearms. An item in the survey asked specifically where respondents had obtained their most recent handgun. Modes of acquisition are displayed in Table 7.3 for that portion of the sample claiming to possess such a gun. Friends and family emerged by far as the primary means of obtaining handguns: combined, 71 percent of the sample cited these two sources. Purchases from gun stores also appeared as a source, with 9 percent of the sample claiming to have gotten their handguns there. (Since all of our respondents were under the age of twenty-one, purchases of this nature would be illegal; some

proportion of those claiming this as a source may have used a confeder-
ate above the age of twenty-one to purchase the gun, and a segment
may also have utilized false identifications.) Street sources, as well as
those involved in drug sales and use, were also mentioned, though to a
considerably lesser degree than family and friends.

Drugs and Guns

We have referred several times to the common stereotype of a link
between gun possession by juveniles and drug-related activity. This
issue is addressed presently in Table 7.4. As it was for the male sample,
drug use is operationalized for females as self-reported use, during the
past two years, of heroin, regular cocaine, or crack (see Chapter 5). The
reported use of such drugs was rare; crack was reported by 1.1 percent
of the females, cocaine by 1.5 percent, and heroin by 1.5 percent. In the
aggregate, only 14 respondents reported having used "hard" drugs.
Greater numbers (9 percent of the sample) reported having sold drugs,
measured in the same manner as for male respondents.

Our findings suggest a link between drug use and gun possession
among our female respondents. Although their numbers were quite small,
more than half of those who reported using "hard" drugs also reported
possessing a firearm; only 5 percent of those who did not use drugs possessed a firearm. None of the students who used drugs carried guns

Table 7.4. Female Respondents' Gun Ownership and Gun Carrying by Drug
and Gang Activity

	Gun ownership		Gun carrying	
	(N)	%	*(N)*	%
Hard-drug use (heroin, cocaine, crack)				
No	(775)	5	(760)	5
Yes	(14)	57*	(12)	0
Drug sales				
No	(601)	9	(611)	7
Yes	(56)	26*	(58)	24*
Gang affiliation				
None	(647)	10	(611)	8
Unstructured gang	(110)	14	(104)	20**
Structured gang	(19)	58***	(19)	58***

* Different from "no," $p < .05$.
** Different from "no gang affiliation," $p < .05$.
*** Different from "unstructured gang," $p < .05$.

(though, again, the small number of persons using drugs in this sample means that little can be said about links between the two). Respondents who sold drugs reported substantially higher levels of gun possession than those who claimed not to have engaged in this practice (26 versus 9 percent) as well as higher levels of gun carrying (24 versus 7 percent).

Gangs and Guns

The role of females in urban gangs seems to be quite different from that of male gang members; females often are only indirect participants in gang-related illegal activities (Campbell 1990; Moore 1991). Consequently, we suspect that, to the extent that a gang-gun relationship holds for females in our sample, it is more a matter of association than of participation in overt gang activity, particularly in its most violent forms.

We employed the same measurement regarding gang membership for female as for male respondents (see Chapter 6). As shown in Table 7.4, a relationship between gang membership and gun possession and carrying is quite apparent for the female students. Of those with no gang affiliation (84 percent of the sample), only 10 percent reported possession of a gun and only 8 percent had carried one. The percentage of unstructured gang members who possessed a gun (14 percent) differed little from that of non–gang members; but those who carried guns (20 percent) greatly exceeded the number of gun carriers among non–gang members. Finally, females who were affiliated with structured gangs were by far the most likely to possess and carry guns (58 percent in both instances).

In sum, it is clear that, though their exposure to a firearm-related environment parallelled that of our male inner-city students, our female students were far less likely to possess and carry guns than were males. Nonetheless, for females who did engage in gun-related activities, the relationships that characterized males held as well for females. Gun possession and carrying were related to the perceived need for protection (even more so than for males), to involvement in drug activity, and to affiliation with gangs (especially more structured ones). These relationships bear watching over the next several years for signs of change. As conditions in the inner city seem to be recruiting more and more young men into firearm-related activity, can we expect to see an increase in young women's involvement in the same activity? Will that increase occur at a faster rate than for males?

Weapon-Related Victimization

The issue of juveniles and guns is set in the larger context of violence perpetrated by and against youth. National victimization survey data indicate that, in 1991, over two million teenagers were the victims of violent crime (U.S. Department of Justice 1992:28; see also Whitaker and Bastion 1991; and Bastion and Taylor 1991:23). On the one hand, most of the violence discovered through the national victimization studies amounted to simple assaults involving minor injuries and committed without the use of weapons. On the other hand, the sense of teen-related violence as generally of lesser seriousness is not easily reconciled with the results of the present study and with popular reports of violence and weapon carrying among teenagers.

In fact, the pictures provided by victimization and weapon-carrying surveys are not necessarily contradictory. It may well be that the transport of weapons by youth does not translate to serious injury to youth. However, it may also be that the victimization studies do not focus, at least in sufficient depth, on the weapon-related victimization of inner-city youth, adolescents thought popularly to experience violence at rates exceeding those of other groups (see Chapter 1). In this vein, the present chapter summarizes the results of an exploration of victimization, not simply through firearms but through knives and other weapons as well, of the male and female students comprising our inner-city high school sample. We have broadened the notion of victimization beyond firearm-related attacks because, theoretically, the independent variables examined here—the dangerous environment and high-risk illegal behaviors —are not gun specific.[2]

Victimization Levels

Students in our sample were asked whether they had experienced any of the following assaults while at school or in transit to or from school in the last few years: shot at with a gun, stabbed with a knife, injured with a weapon other than a gun or a knife. Limitation of victimization incidents to those at or associated with travel to and from school necessarily produces a conservative portrait of students' violent experiences. School tends to aggregate youth in a fashion that increases the odds of disputes. However, it also constrains the amount and types of violence that emerge from such conflict. It is assumed that any relationships described here would increase in magnitude were the focus on violence away from school.

For each of the three victimization items, response categories included never (0), just once (1), a few times (2), and many times (3). Combining responses to the victimization items permits the calculation of a victimization score for each respondent ranging from 0 (never victimized) to 9 (shot at, stabbed, and otherwise injured many times each). Table 7.5 displays patterns of victimization by sex. Two in ten students had had a victimization score of at least 1. Males (30 percent) were

Table 7.5.   Weapon-Related Victimization Profiles[a]

Victimization	Total (%)	Males (%)	Females (%)
Shot at	12	20	6
(N)	(1380)	(592)	(733)
Stabbed	8	10	7
(N)	(1378)	(591)	(734)
Injured with other weapon type	13	17	10
(N)	(1374)	(590)	(730)
Victimization Score			
0	79	70	84
1	9	11	8
2	5	8	3
3+	7	11	5
(N)	(1363)	(583)	(727)

[a] N in parentheses represents sample and subsample populations upon which percentages are based. All differences between males and females reported are statistically significant at least at the .05 level.

twice as likely as females (16 percent) to have been attacked. More than half of those assaulted had experienced multiple victimizations. Type of weapon used in the assaults varied. Students were as likely to have been shot at as injured with a weapon other than a gun or a knife; the odds of having been stabbed were somewhat lower. Higher percentages of males than of females reported shootings. Females most likely were victimized with a weapon other than a gun or knife.

Dangerous Environments

Attention to the life-styles or routine activities of victims of violent crime has become a staple of much analysis of victimization patterns (Miethe, Stafford, and Long 1987; Felson 1994). In brief, students of the issue argue that the occurrence of a crime reflects the coincidence of a motivated offender, a suitable target, and the absence of capable guardians against predation (Felson 1987). All else equal, persons whose routine activities place them in locations more likely frequented by offenders and less well policed than other places stand the better chance of becoming victims of such crimes as robbery and assault.

Many of the victim's activities studied by researchers in this vein are derivative of demographic status; youth and single persons, for example, are at greater risk simply by virtue of life-styles that take them out of the home and into more trafficked areas, thus increasing their level of exposure as potential targets of violence (Miethe et al. 1987). Association with members of demographic categories disproportionately populated with predators (e.g., young males) increases the likelihood of victimization (Lauritsen, Laub, and Sampson 1992). Victimization for these individuals is more or less random within the categories to which they belong. Apart from these social-category-based activities, certain behavioral choices may put one at higher risk of victimization: accepting rides with strangers, frequenting dangerous bars, walking alone at night in parks, and so forth.

As we noted (for males only) in Chapter 2, many students in the present study were exposed to dangerous environments. Four in ten (39 percent; 37 percent of the males and 42 percent of the females) reported that male relatives carried guns outside their homes. One in three (35 percent; 42 percent of the males and 28 percent of the females) had friends who carried guns outside the home. One in four (23 percent; males and females equally) considered guns easy to get in their neighborhoods. Eighty percent of the respondents, males and females equally, reported that other students carried weapons to school. Sixty-six percent of the respondents (again, males and females alike) personally knew someone who had done so. Two-thirds also personally knew someone who had been shot at, stabbed, or otherwise assaulted while in school. Finally, a third of the respondents (38 percent; 35 percent of males and 41 percent of females) agreed or strongly agreed—as opposed to disagreeing strongly or otherwise—that "there is a lot of violence in this school."

High-Risk Illegal Activities

Nothing in any explication of the routine activities approach specifies that the activities in question must be legal. Indeed, Jensen and Brownfield (1986), Lauritsen, Sampson, and Laub (1991), and Sheley et al. (1992) have argued persuasively that a victim's high-risk routine activities as easily can be *illegal* as legal. That is, routinely engaging in illegal activities (e.g., drug transactions or robberies) or belonging to groups that routinely engage in or attract violence (sometimes proactively, as do certain youth gangs) would seem to place individuals in exceptionally high-risk categories.

As noted earlier, many students in the present sample reported engaging in behaviors that likely increased the risk of violent victimization: criminal activity, drug use and trafficking, gang activity. Twenty-seven percent of the respondents (42 percent of males and 14 percent of females) reported having been arrested or picked up by the police at least once; 2 percent (6 percent of males, 1 percent of females) had been arrested or picked up "many" times. Fifteen percent (23 percent of males, 9 percent of females) reported having stolen something worth at least $50. Five percent (9 percent of males, less than 1 percent of females) reported using a weapon to commit a crime. Use of hard drugs was reported by 4 percent (7 percent of males, 2 percent of females). A greater percentage of students (13 percent; 18 percent for males and 9 percent for females) had either themselves dealt drugs or worked for someone who did. Nineteen percent of the students (22 percent of the males, 16 percent of the females) were affiliated with a gang of some kind.

One in four students (males and females roughly equally) reported carrying a weapon while in school, and more than four in ten (44 percent; 51 percent of males and 38 percent of females) carried a weapon outside school. Whether or not weapon carrying by the students was proactive (related to criminality, for example) or reactive (fear-driven), it can be hypothesized reasonably that the behavior raised the stakes in disputes that otherwise might have been settled nonviolently, leaving all parties at higher risk of injury.

Who Is Victimized?

At least among inner-city students of the kind sampled in this study, sociodemographic characteristics are not highly predictive of violent victimization. Victimization status generally, as well as reports of shootings, stabbings, and other injuries treated separately, differed insignificantly among respondents across racial and ethnic lines, age categories, and grade levels. Only sex seemed to influence victimization levels. For each type of victimization and for victimization generally, males were statistically significantly more likely to have experienced an assault.

As the findings in Table 7.6 suggest, exposure to a dangerous environment significantly raises the risk of weapon-related victimization for students of the type studied here. Since the same results pertained for victimization status generally as for each victimization item separately, only relationships regarding the former are reported in the table. Respondents with male relatives who carried guns were more likely than those without such relatives to have been violently victimized. Those whose friends carried guns and those who perceived guns as readily available in the neighborhood also were more likely to report assaults. Students who reported that their peers carried weapons to school and who personally knew other students who had done so were more likely to report having been victimized. Higher percentages of those who personally knew other students who had been shot at, stabbed, or

Table 7.6. Dangerous Environment and Weapon-Related Victimization[a]

	Victimization score (%)			
Item	0	1	2	3+
Male relatives carry guns (1329)				
No	85*	8	3	3
Yes	67	10	8	14
Friends carry guns (1310)				
No	85*	8	3	4
Yes	65	10	10	15
Guns accessible in neighborhood (1252)				
No	86*	6	3	4
Yes	72	11	7	10
Peers carry weapons to school (1314)				
No more than a few	87*	7	4	3
More than a few	73	11	6	10
Personally know kids who carry weapons to school (1323)				
No	82*	8	5	5
Yes	67	11	6	16
Personally know kids victimized with weapons at school (1363)				
No	90*	6	2	2
Yes	68	11	8	12
Violence level high in school (1211)				
Disagree	81	9	5	5
Agree	77	8	5	10

[a] N in parentheses.
* $p < .001$.

otherwise injured in school reported assaults. Of all the measures of environment, only the perception of one's school as violent was not linked to victimization status.

Given the findings regarding environment, those reported in Table 7.7 concerning higher-risk activities are not surprising. Again, since the same results pertained for victimization status generally as for each victimization item separately, only relationships regarding the former are reported in the table. Criminal activity increases the risk of weapon-related victimization. Those with arrest records, those who had stolen something worth at least fifty dollars, and those who had used a weapon to commit a crime were more likely to have been victimized. So also were those who reported carrying weapons in and out of school, using hard drugs, selling drugs, and belonging to a gang.[3]

Table 7.7. High-Risk Activities and Weapon-Related Victimization[a]

	Victimization Score (%)			
Item	0	1	2	3+
Arrest record (1331)				
No	87*	7	4	3
Yes	60	14	7	19
Theft worth $50+ (1336)				
No	83*	8	4	5
Yes	59	11	10	20
Used weapon in crime (1363)				
No	80*	9	5	6
Yes	71	6	6	17
Carried weapon to and from school (1363)				
No	84*	8	4	4
Yes	61	13	9	17
Carried weapon while out of school (1363)				
No	89*	7	3	1
Yes	64	12	9	15
Used hard drugs (1363)				
No	80*	9	5	6
Yes	40	9	11	40
Sold drugs (1259)				
No	84*	8	4	5
Yes	50	16	9	24
Gang member (1349)				
No	83*	8	5	4
Yes	61	13	8	19

[a] N in parentheses.
* $p < .001$.

Multivariate Considerations

Few of the variables examined in this study as potentially linked to weapon-related victimization are uncorrelated with the others. It is possible, then, that most of the relationships reported in Tables 7.6 and 7.7 actually simply echo others; many may be reduced to a few. To test this possibility, multivariate analysis was conducted to assess the relationship between any given independent variable and violent victimization score net of the effects of other independent variables.[4]

As the findings displayed in Table 7.8 indicate, and as our bivariate analyses suggested earlier, sex is the only sociodemographic variable related to weapon-related victimization; males are more likely to be victims of violence. The dangerous environment *outside school* is related to violent victimization, but the dangerous environment *inside school* is less obviously related. Independent of the effects of other variables, personal acquaintance with those who carry weapons to school and perceiving one's school as a violent place are not linked to victimization (perhaps indicating rational decisions to maintain a low profile in the dangerous environment). Only personal acquaintance with those who have been victimized in school is related to victimization level (perhaps suggesting the possibility of simultaneous victimization of respondent and friends). High-risk activities, for the most part, increase the likelihood that a student will experience weapon-related victimization. Net of the effects of the other variables, only drug-related activity (drug selling and hard-drug use) is not related to the victimization of students of the type surveyed in this study.

In sum, while hardly universal and perhaps even surprisingly infrequent given common stereotypes about inner-city life, weapon-related

Table 7.8. TOBIT Coefficients Relating Victimization Score to Sociodemographic Characteristics, Dangerous Environment, and High-Risk Illegal Activities

Independent variables	Victimization score
Sociodemographic	
Sex	1.090**
Age	−.067
Race/ethnicity[a]	
Black	−.431
Hispanic	−.680
Dangerous environment	
Male relatives carry guns	.363*
Guns accessible in neighborhood	.274*
Personally know kids who carry weapons to school	.161
Violence level high in school	.014
Personally know kids victimized at school	.213**
High-risk illegal activities	
Arrest record	.803**
Carried weapon while out of school	.472*
Sold drugs	.424
Gang member	.669**
Constant	2.993

* $p < .05$.　　** $p < .001$.
[a] Other races and ethnic groups comprise reference category.

victimization is not uncommon among inner-city high school students—in the present study, among students in particularly troubled inner-city schools. One in five students (nearly one in three males) among the current respondents had been shot at, stabbed, or otherwise injured with a weapon at or in transit to or from school in the last few years. One in ten had been so victimized more than once.

Many students in the present sample reported engaging in behaviors that likely increased the risk of violent victimization: criminal activity, drug use and trafficking, gang activity, the carrying of weapons. Most such behaviors were linked to victimization level. At the multivariate level, criminal activity, gang membership, and the carrying of weapons all increased the likelihood of violent victimization. Net of the effects of the other variables presently studied, drug-related activity (relatively rare among the respondents) had no impact on the chances of victimization.

Importantly, at the multivariate level, dangerous environment *outside* the school, as opposed to dangerous environment *in* school, was the better predictor of weapon-related victimization at or during travel to and from school. Judging from the present findings (and recognizing that the present respondents are students in particularly troubled schools), it appears that schools do not generate weapon-related violence as much as they represent the location where violence spawned outside the institution is played out (see Parker et al. 1991). That is, inner-city youth do not assume new personas upon passing through school gates. Most weapon-related violence in schools is imported and occurs because the social worlds of some students encourage use of weapons (students see males in their families carrying guns, for example), because some pupils engage in behaviors known to perpetuate violence (criminal activity, for example), or because simply carrying weapons promotes more injurious outcomes of standard juvenile disputes.

Given these findings, it cannot be assumed that increased security within schools will reduce the weapon-related victimization levels of students. It must be remembered that the schools represented in the present study have histories of violence and maintain considerable security. As well, little difference has been found in rates of violent victimization in schools with and without conventional security measures such as patrolled hallways and visitor checks-ins (Bastion and Taylor 1991). This is not to suggest that school administrators should abandon all efforts at safer schools. Indeed, it is assumed that differences in administrations, teachers, and physical layouts are linked to differential rates of violence across school sites. But, no matter the differential, the *source* of trouble lies outside the school, and schools are more likely to displace than to reduce violence. Reduction in the levels of violence against students, as opposed to reduction of violence on school grounds, will follow only after the external conditions promoting the violence are addressed.

Guns in the Suburbs[5]

To this date, studies of juveniles and guns, including our own, have focused either on urban youth or on nationally representative samples that blur urban and nonurban distinctions. Only one study (Sadowski et al. 1989) cited in this book pertains directly to nonurban youth. Unfortunately its sample is highly select, and the report of findings does not distinguish suburban from rural respondents.

However, a considerable body of anecdotal evidence points to the spread of firearms beyond city limits and into the hands of *suburban* juveniles (*Chicago Tribune* 1992; *Washington Post* 1992; *Newsweek* 1992; *Time* 1993; *U.S. News and World Report* 1993). To the extent that this is the case, it necessitates a reconceptualization of the "kids and guns" problem: no longer can we portray juvenile firearm activity, at least exclusively, as a reflection of urban poverty.

Research Site

This section describes the first systematic empirical study specifically of a suburban population of juveniles. The study was conducted in Jefferson Parish, Louisiana. Jefferson Parish borders the city of New Orleans on the west. Its approximately 450,000 residents place it one-hundredth among the nation's 3,319 counties. It is classically suburban, comprised of little industry and nearly entirely of housing developments, apartment complexes, and shopping centers. Predominantly white (78 percent), it is the wealthiest of Louisiana's parishes and is known statewide as a "white-flight" area (since 1960, its general population has more than doubled, while New Orleans's has decreased and become increasingly African-American). Like most suburban areas, Jefferson Parish has a low crime rate relative to its adjacent urban neighbor and has experienced little gang activity.[6]

Admittedly, no single suburban locale is "representative" of all such locales; what are labeled suburbs in America display considerable variation, perhaps more than what we term cities. Nonetheless, Jefferson Parish does not appear unusual in any obvious way. Its 1990 per capita income stood at $12,845, with a median household income of $27,916. Of the adult population, 76 percent have a high school diploma or some college education; 19 percent have college degrees. Two-thirds of the population is in the labor force; unemployment in recent years has averaged about seven percent. Twenty-seven percent of the parish's population is under eighteen years of age.

Sample

Representative samples of students in three of Jefferson Parish's seven public high schools were surveyed in the spring of 1993.[7] Importantly, school affiliation had no influence on any finding reported below. The number of respondents for this survey ultimately totaled 432:133 from one school, 139 from a second, and 160 from the third. Conservatively, 14 cases were excluded from analysis (leaving 418 cases) because the respondents failed to answer more than five of the questionnaire items. Missing cases in the analyses to follow average only 1.62% per item.[8]

The sample contained nearly equal numbers of males (48 percent) and females (52 percent). Sixty-six percent of the respondents were white and 21 percent black. The remaining respondents were Hispanic, Asian, and "other"; these respondents, 13 percent of the total, have been combined into a single category: "other." Sixty-six percent of the students were in the tenth grade, and 34 percent were in the eleventh. Finally, only one-fifth of the respondents were under sixteen years of age (modal age = 16; mean age = 16.27).

Firearm Activity

Table 7.9 offers descriptive data for each firearm-activity measure employed in this study. Students were asked whether or not they presently possessed (a) a revolver (regular handgun) and (b) an automatic or semi-automatic handgun. Thirteen percent of the respondents owned or possessed a revolver and 9 percent an automatic or semiautomatic handgun

Table 7.9. Gender and Race/Ethnicity Effects on Firearm Activity[a] (%)

Variable	Total (418)	Male (200)	Female (218)	Black (88)	White (274)	Other (55)
Owns revolver	12.9	19.5	6.9**	8.0	16.8	1.8*
Owns automatic or semiautomatic	9.1	16.5	2.3**	10.2	9.1	5.5
Carries a gun	17.2	27.6	7.8**	14.8	19.8	7.3

[a] Measurement described in text (N in parentheses).
* $p < .01$.   ** $p < .001$.

at the time of the survey. Eighteen percent of the total sample owned at least one type of handgun (4 percent owned both types). Respondents also were asked whether or not they carried a gun outside their homes, including in their cars (0 = no; 1 = yes). Seventeen percent reported engaging in this behavior. Of the total number of respondents who reported engaging in ownership or in gun carrying (99), only 47 percent had done both.

In addition to descriptive data for the entire sample, Table 7.9 provides sex and race differences regarding firearm activity.[9] Males clearly were more actively involved in all of the behaviors examined here. White students were more likely to own revolvers, though race otherwise was unrelated to participation in gun activities.

Drug and Criminal Activity

Only 4 percent of the respondents reported heroin, cocaine, or crack use "during the past year"; 7 percent had been "involved in dealing heroin, cocaine, or crack either as a seller or working for a seller." Twelve percent of the respondents had either used or sold heroin, cocaine, or crack at least once during the past year. Six percent of the students during the past year had "committed a crime with a weapon." At the bivariate level, both drug activity and violent criminality were statistically significantly related to both gun ownership and gun carrying.

Dangerous Environment[10]

To assess the extent to which respondents perceived their social environments to be dangerous, they were asked whether or not in the past year they had been threatened with a gun ("never," "just once," "a few times," and "many times"). Twenty-three percent had been so threatened; 12 percent at least a few times.[11] Additionally, 40 percent of the students during the past year had attended parties (or other recreational events) at which guns had been fired.[12] As well, respondents were asked how often, on an average day and when not in school, they feared a violent attack. Eighty-one percent "never" or "rarely" felt fearful; 13 percent "sometimes" experienced such fear; and 6 percent were afraid "often." Finally, respondents were asked the likelihood that, by age twenty-five, they personally will have been shot. Most (83 percent) considered the possibility "very unlikely" or "unlikely"; 12 percent thought it "likely," and 5 percent "very likely."[13] At the bivariate level, only one of the dangerous-environment indicators (fear of attack) was not statistically significantly related to both gun ownership and gun carrying.

Multivariate Considerations

Moderate interrelationships among many of the independent variables suggested the need for multivariate analysis.[14] Table 7.10 displays logistic regression results describing the relation of ownership of a revolver to the demographic and independent variables of interest in this study. Table 7.11 duplicates presentation of this analysis after substituting ownership of an automatic or semiautomatic handgun as the dependent variable.

An examination of the findings in the tables indicates that ownership

Table 7.10 Logistic Regression of Selected Variables on Ownership of a Revolver[a]

Variables	Total	Males	Females
Demographic variables			
Sex (female omitted)			
Male	.8204*		
	(.3492)		
Race (other omitted)			
White	2.5587*	8.0661	1.4012
	(1.0479)	(19.6320)	(1.1466)
Black	1.1140	6.7631	−.1887
	(1.1231)	(19.6370)	(1.4956)
Drug activity	.7451	.7763	.6451
	(.4406)	(.5203)	(.8533)
Violent criminality	.5442	.3648	1.1781
	(.5553)	(.6693)	(1.0068)
Dangerous environment			
Threatened with a gun	.3368	.3957	.2413
	(.1867)	(.2179)	(.4079)
Guns fired at social events	.3145	.2555	.3520
	(.1988)	(.2409)	(.3582)
Fears violent attack	−.3302	−.4232	−.1892
	(.2123)	(.2812)	(.3346)
Fears being shot by age 25	−.0316	−.0948	.1552
	(.2009)	(.2475)	(.3512)
Constant	−5.1487***	−9.5387	−4.5897**
	(1.1689)	(19.6432)	(1.3256)
Likelihood ratio χ^2	49.860***	27.596**	11.580
Degrees of freedom	9	8	8
N	411	196	215

[a] Standard errors in parentheses.
* $p < .05$.   ** $p < .01$.   *** $p < .001$.

Table 7.11. Logistic Regression of Selected Variables on Ownership of Automatic or Semiautomatic Handgun[a]

Variables	Total	Males	Females
Demographic variables			
Sex (female omitted)			
Male	1.8919**		
	(.5585)		
Race (other omitted)			
White	.4821	1.7312	−1.3191
Black	(.6907)	(1.1247)	(1.2223)
	.0800	1.3258	−8.8029
	(.7895)	(1.1797)	(61.0015)
Drug activity	.5041	.3667	1.3711
	(.4934)	(.5388)	(1.9870)
Violent criminality	1.1558*	1.4087*	−9.4562
	(.5745)	(.6247)	(168.4740)
Dangerous environment			
Threatened with a gun	.2802	.0603	1.6327*
	(.2166)	(.2348)	(.7386)
Guns fired at social events	.3163	.4194	−.1867
	(.2261)	(.2451)	(.8257)
Fears violent attack	−.4318	−.2579	−.7050
	(.2719)	(.2928)	(.8913)
Fears being shot by age 25	.1694	.1965	−.2529
	(.2330)	(.2565)	(.8756)
Constant	−4.8786***	−4.3242**	−3.9115*
	(.9967)	(1.3378)	(1.7573)
Likelihood ratio χ^2	50.971***	23.310**	14.395
Degrees of freedom	9	8	8
N	411	196	215

[a] Standard errors in parentheses.
* $p < .05$.   ** $p < .01$.   *** $p < .001$.

of either type of handgun is related to sex of the respondent. As well, net of the effects of other variables, whites are more likely than members of other racial and ethnic categories to possess a revolver, though not an automatic or semiautomatic handgun. Beyond this, while none of the independent variables is related to ownership of a revolver, possession of an automatic or semiautomatic handgun is associated, for males, with violent criminality and, for females, with having been threatened with a gun.[15]

Logistic regression results regarding gun carrying are presented in Table 7.12. As with gun ownership, sex and race of the respondent

Table 7.12. Logistic Regression of Selected Variables on Gun Carrying[a]

Variables	Total	Males	Females
Demographic variables			
Sex (Female omitted)			
Male	1.0477**		
	(.3477)		
Race (other)			
White	1.4323*	1.1758	1.7720
	(.6432)	(.7805)	(1.1741)
Black	.3920	.3858	−.1805
	(.7349)	(.8970)	(1.5225)
Drug activity	1.2390**	1.2977**	1.0865
	(.4327)	(.5207)	(.8236)
Violent criminality	1.7217**	2.3162**	.4347
	(.5652)	(.7591)	(1.0666)
Dangerous environment			
Threatened with a gun	.5387**	.6455**	.5391
	(.1817)	(.2200)	(.3828)
Guns fired at social events	.3547	.2377	.6763
	(.1884)	(.2317)	(.3455)
Fears violent attack	−.1709	−.1696	−.3040
	(.2024)	(.2628)	(.3422)
Fears being shot by age 25	.1582	−.1684	.6692*
	(.1948)	(.2520)	(.3332)
Constant	−5.1584***	−3.3119**	−6.5576***
	(.8348)	(.9933)	(1.4940)
Likelihood ratio χ^2	101.977***	53.757***	30.086
Degrees of freedom	9	8	8
N	410	195	215

[a] Standard errors in parentheses.
* $p < .05$.   ** $p < .01$.   *** $p < .001$.

influence gun carrying net of the effects of other variables. Beyond this, however, the picture differs considerably from that regarding gun ownership. Students—especially males—who carry guns are more likely to be involved in drug activity and more likely to have committed crimes with weapons. For males, dangerous environment has little to do with gun carrying; only having been threatened with a gun (likely, given the presumed life-styles of those involved in drug trafficking and violent criminal activity) is related to the dependent variable. Gun carrying (much less frequent among females) is linked among females only to the perception that the respondent is likely to suffer a gunshot wound by age twenty-five.[16]

Implications

Are guns showing up in the hands of suburban juveniles to any great extent? To the extent our findings are generalizable, it seems so.[17] The numbers of students in this study reporting gun ownership and carrying are significant—at least relative to those found in our inner-city study and to those reported in the investigations cited in this book. Nearly one in five Jefferson Parish students owned a handgun. Better than one in four males (28 percent) owned such a gun. Comparable figures for gun carrying in this suburban sample are one in six (17 percent) for the whole sample and one in four (28 percent) for males.

Contrast these findings with those reported in a study of high school juniors in the city (not the suburbs) of Seattle: 11 percent of the males reported owning a handgun; six percent had carried a gun to school sometime in the past (Callahan and Rivara 1992). As well, one in six male students in our inner-city sample reported owning an automatic or semiautomatic handgun; one in seven owned a revolver; one in three carried a gun at least occasionally.

If our findings are representative of suburbs as a whole (as yet undetermined definitively), we can no longer conceptualize the problem of guns in the hands of juveniles as an urban phenomenon. Firearm activity by suburban youth either has gone undetected while we concentrated on urban gun activity, or (more likely) firearms more recently have found their way into the hands of suburban youth. The present data afford us no indication of the relationship, if any exists, between urban and suburban firearm patterns; i.e., we cannot know whether suburban adolescent firearm activity reflects the latest wave of an urban dispersion process. We cannot determine the character of the first juveniles to become suburban gun possessors or the age of those youths. It is unlikely that the firearm activity was drug or crime related—at least judging by the low percentage of youth in the present sample who participated in such behaviors. However, whatever its source, it is clear that firearm activity has spread well into the juvenile population of the suburban area in question.

Why are adolescents becoming armed in the suburbs? This book and other research locate the source of gun activity among contemporary urban youth in their perception that their social environment is hostile. Though bivariate results point to such a link in the present sample, multivariate results do not. Those who owned handguns did not inhabit discernibly more hostile environments than did nonowners—beyond the danger that characterized the violent criminality of owners of automatic or semiautomatic weapons. Nor were those who carried handguns more likely the products of dangerous surroundings, net of involvement in drug and criminal activity.

Since criminality and drug activity characterized only a minority of gun possessors and carriers, what motivated the firearm activity of the majority if not self-protection? Though our urban youth and serious juvenile offenders rather clearly were not motivated to possess guns for purposes of status enhancement, perhaps suburban youth were. This would suggest some form of subculture (however amorphous) of segments of suburban youth whereby status is accrued through gun possession, and the spread of firearms among juveniles reflects imitation or contagion. The public vocabularies of motive underlying such behaviors probably center more on self-protection than on overt efforts to enhance status, but the private evaluation of one's environment as dangerous or safe need not correspond to one's publicly stated evaluation. We have no data by which to investigate these possibilities, so they remain purely speculative. Nonetheless, whether grounded in status enhancement or otherwise, to the extent that gun possession and carrying increase among suburban adolescents, we can expect to observe an escalation of ownership, transport, and use of firearms for "protective" purposes.

Conclusions

It is clear that the problem of the acquisition of firearms by juveniles in the main is an urban, male phenomenon. Inner-city females—at least those of the type looked at in this study—seem little involved in gun-related activity relative to males; suburban females—judging by our limited sample—are even less involved in such behaviors. We do not mean, however, to characterize the issue of females and guns as trivial. One of every twenty female students in our sample, after all, claimed ownership of an automatic or semiautomatic handgun. Nearly the same number reported carrying a gun most or all of the time; another 8 percent did so at least occasionally.

If young, inner-city women obtain and carry guns for protection, then it is very possible that the ownership and carrying numbers we have found here will increase over time. Protection seems to be defined in terms of the likelihood that others are armed and therefore dangerous even in minor disputes. Large numbers of males in the social environments of these young women carry guns routinely. Not insignificant numbers of females do too. Absent the introduction of serious guardianship into those environments, the move toward arming oneself seems as logical a response for females as for males.

Of course, the tragedy of this response lies in the fact that behaviors such as carrying weapons seem to increase rather than decrease the likelihood of violent victimization. Our analysis of the victimization reports of our inner-city respondents demonstrates clearly that the carrying of weapons is linked to violent victimization independent of whether or not an individual occupies a dangerous environment or engages in criminal, drug, or gang activities—all of which (save drug activity) also independently raise one's risk of victimization.

What we have seen in the inner city, we might also soon see in the suburbs. Again, we stress that our study of guns in the hands of suburban juveniles was exploratory. To the extent that its findings are generalizable, we have learned that, at least in some suburban neighborhoods, male adolescents now find guns a significant part of their social worlds. It seems that suburban gun-related activity is not yet sufficiently dispersed to prompt "protective" carrying of guns (though protection is commonly cited as motive), but the same process that drives the gun-related behaviors of inner-city youth probably will take hold in the suburbs as well. There is likely a level of gun possession that, once achieved, motivates yet more possession. That escalation, almost by definition, raises the "necessity" of acquisition and carrying of firearms by others. Suburban youth may not have reached the precipitating level yet, since dangerous environment, net of other factors, is unrelated to their firearm activity. But for each suburban youth who succumbs to the lure of status attainment through gun possession, the suburban "protective" arms race draws nearer.

Notes

1. Parts of this section are taken from Smith and Sheley (1995).
2. With few exceptions, findings pertaining to victimization through our aggregated measure of weaponry pertain as well to victimization through firearms alone.
3. Gang members who belonged to unstructured gangs were more susceptible to violent victimization than were non–gang members but less susceptible than were members of structured gangs.
4. The specific multivariate technique employed in this analysis was TOBIT (McDonald and Moffitt 1980), employed because the dependent variable has a high proportion of its cases (79 percent) clustered at a limiting value (zero or "no victimization"). The high degree of intercorrelation among the independent variables in the present study necessitated the analysis of many TOBIT models, alternating highly related variables from model to model. Essentially the same patterns emerged with each model. For those unfamiliar with TOBIT procedures, what is

important in the present context is whether a given coefficient is statistically significant.

5.   Parts of this section are taken from Sheley and Brewer (1995).

6.   As the findings of this study were being analyzed, Jefferson Parish recorded its first incident of a public high school teacher being shot by a student—in this instance, a fourteen-year-old boy upset over a change in the classroom seating arrangement.

7.   The three schools from which students were sampled were selected on the basis of their academic profiles. That is, Jefferson Parish high schools were divided into thirds (two schools in the top and bottom thirds, three in the middle third) based on the percentage of their students scoring above the fiftieth percentile on the California Achievement Test (CAT); one school was chosen from each third. Principals in each of the schools provided access to as random a sample of sophomores and juniors in attendance on a given day as was practically possible. In two schools, this meant distribution of the questionnaire in randomly chosen English classes required of all students. In the third school, students were surveyed in their homerooms (mandatory for all students) at randomly chosen times. In short, all sophomores and juniors in attendance theoretically had the same chance to be included in the sample. Attendance in two schools on the day of administration was roughly 90 percent, and in the third, roughly 70 percent. In each school in which respondents were surveyed, over 95 percent of the students who were addressed by the researchers chose to participate in the study.

8.   As they did for our larger study of inner-city youth and incarcerated juveniles, attempts to establish the level of reliability in the present study centered on pairs of items, the responses to which were checked for logical consistency. For example, respondents who claimed never to carry a gun should not have identified, in a later item, their reason for carrying a gun. Four such pairs of items were examined. Inconsistent responses averaged only 1.4 percent within a range of .5 to 3.4 percent. To determine how systematic were the inconsistencies, we scored each respondent on number of inconsistent answers; respondents could receive scores between 0 and 4. Only one respondent scored above 1, and that case received a score of 2.

Validity was more difficult to assess, absent official records against which to compare the self-report data. However, seeking construct validation, we note that respondents who reported committing a crime with a weapon also were more likely to have been arrested ($r = .339$). Those reporting drug use were also more likely than those who did not to have been arrested and to have committed a crime with a weapon ($r = .307$ and .289, respectively). Respondents involved in drug dealing also were more likely to have been arrested ($r = .325$) and to have committed a crime with a weapon ($r = .269$).

9.   Respondent's school affiliation (see above), age, and grade level were unrelated to these same variables and are not reported in Table 7.9.

10.   In the context of a cross-sectional survey, treatment of the dangerous environment as an independent variable poses problems. We cannot ascertain definitively, for example, whether the absence of a link between fear of attack and gun possession indicates no actual association or a decrease in fear *after* the acquisition of a gun. Nor can we be sure whether being threatened with a gun increases the likelihood of carrying a gun or vice versa. Recognizing that we cannot eliminate this problem, we have attempted nonetheless to blunt its impact through use of four different types of indicators of dangerous environment: One measures fear, two address events that suggest high risk of violence, and the fourth characterizes the environment in terms of the respondent's self-assessed prospects for violent victimization. In the final analysis, of course, the issue of which came first—danger or firearm—matters less than the issue of the association of dangerous environment with gun possession. If the two are linked, then policy must address that link.

11.   Importantly, this item does not distinguish type of threat. It is unclear whether, for example, the respondent had been personally and directly threatened with a gun or had been more generally threatened—as a member of group at whom a gun was pointed.

12.   Since schoolmates socialize with each other so often, we assume that the events in question number fewer than the number of students citing them. The exact number cannot be estimated presently. Since school affiliation is unrelated to any of the findings discussed here, we are able to state that the percentage of students attending recreational events of the type in question here is not a function of problematic activity by the students of one school.

13.   The four measures indexing "dangerous environment" vary in their relationships to each other (r ranges from .049 to .373) and do not scale ($\alpha = .516$). Sex was related to responses to each of the items indexing dangerous environment. Females registered greater fear of violent attack, but males were more likely to have been threatened with a gun, to have attended social events at which shots had been fired, and to judge themselves vulnerable to being shot by age twenty-five. With one exception (African-American students were more likely than others to have attended social events where shots had been fired), sociodemographic characteristics beyond sex were unassociated with responses to indicators of dangerous environment.

14.   For example, violent criminality is significantly related to involvement in drug activity ($r = .306$), to attendance at social events at which guns were fired ($r = .263$), and to having been threatened with a gun ($r = .212$). Having been threatened with a gun is linked to attendance at social events at which guns were fired ($r = .373$) and to fear of being shot by age 25 ($r = .342$).

15.   The picture is largely the same when we combine types of gun ownership into a single variable: ownership of at least one handgun of either type. Again, males and whites are more likely than their respective counterparts to own a handgun. For females, having been threatened with a gun increases the odds of gun ownership. For males, however, criminality is not associated with gun ownership but, in this instance, attendance at social events where guns have been fired is.

16.   Removal of this variable from the equation results in the transformation of the association between attendance at social events and gun carrying from statistically insignificant (though barely so) to statistically significant. This seems to reflect a life-style pattern. Among females, those who attend such social events also are likely to perceive themselves as vulnerable to being shot. This differs from an overall sense of fear of being violently attacked and need not suggest that anyone has threatened the respondent directly with a gun. Instead, the respondent whose life-style involves dangerous settings likely views herself as someday being in a situation necessitating the use of the gun she carries.

17.   No attempt was made to sample students who were not in attendance on the day the survey was administered nor to sample high school dropouts in the parish. Assuming correlations between absence and behavioral problems and between dropping out and behavioral problems, however, we would argue that the findings reported below represent somewhat conservative estimates of the behaviors and attitudes of interest in this study.

8

KIDS, GUNS, AND VIOLENCE:
CONCLUSIONS AND IMPLICATIONS

[W]e as a society are doing a very poor job at protecting our youth. If we don't get guns off the streets and change our criminal justice system, we risk losing a whole generation of kids.

—U.S. Rep. Charles Schumer of New York, commenting on victimization survey findings, "Young People Are Victimized Most," *New York Times*

The contemporary discussion of juvenile crime is dominated by the imagery of guns, drugs, gangs, and wanton violence. As the rates of crime and violence committed by and against juveniles have increased, the imagery has become progressively more alarmist and terrifying. The "troubled teens" of a decade or two ago have been transformed in media and scholarly accounts into roving bands of well-armed marauders spraying bullets indiscriminately at all who venture near. For all the media copy these themes and images command, there has been relatively little previous research concerning where, how, and why juveniles acquire, carry, and use guns. The research reported here was designed to provide some reliable, quantitative information on these topics.

Our assessment has centered on two critical groups: criminally active juveniles currently incarcerated in state reformatories and inner-city youth in ten urban high schools. Both these groups represent extreme cases. The average criminally active juvenile is probably not nearly as active or as violent as were the juveniles who are now incarcerated for their crimes; and likewise, students in ten of the nation's more troubled urban high schools are certainly not "representative" of high school students in general or even of central-city public high school students in particular. Thus, the depiction of youth crime and violence that emerges from our study is doubtlessly more ominous than it would be had we surveyed a nationally representative sample of inner-city teens.

Still, while ours is not a probability sample of juveniles or of criminally active juveniles, we think it is a fair sampling of the juvenile vio-

147

lence *problem*. Our findings are not radically at odds with those of other studies of the topic; also, as the material in Chapter 7 suggests, problems that only a few years ago were concentrated in "troubled" inner-city high schools have begun to spread noticeably into once-safe neighborhoods and communities. Thus, while the results we have reported do not generalize in the statistical sense to larger or wider populations, they may well be pointing to what is to come for those larger populations.

Among the many findings reported here, which ones are most relevant to public policy issues? First, we have learned that owning and carrying guns were fairly common behaviors in both our samples. About nine of every ten inmates had owned a gun at some time. Fifty-five percent had carried a gun routinely before being incarcerated. One in five male students possessed a gun during the period of our survey; one in three had access to a gun; 12 percent carried guns routinely. Thus, while these behaviors are by no means universal, least of all among the student sample, neither are they unusual. In the inner-city neighborhoods from which our respondents are drawn, firearms seem to have become part of the landscape, one among the many cheerless realities of daily existence.

The evident implication of these findings is that the problem of juvenile violence seems not to be confined to a small group of deviant "bad apples." Violence and the means by which it is perpetrated, rather, have come to be widespread in the impoverished inner city and may be spreading outward. Indeed, a leading concern voiced by many observers of the contemporary urban scene is that violent behavior has become culturally *normative* in the context of underclass life (Auletta 1983; Devine and Wright 1993; Harrington 1984; Jencks and Peterson 1991; Rose and McClain 1990; Wilson 1987). We are left, then, pondering whether we should attempt to control the flow of guns to juveniles or to attack the conditions producing gun-related behaviors. Controlling the flow of guns—"cracking down" on guns is the colloquial phrase—is a euphemism for enacting stricter gun control laws, increasing penalties for juveniles caught carrying guns, and disrupting the flow of arms traffic among youth. Policy discussions of conditions that generate violence generally focus attention on drugs and gangs as youth problems and on the larger issue of poverty and the underclass in this country. Let us consider gun control efforts first.

Controlling Guns

Much of the recent policy debate over firearms has concerned the wisdom of banning ownership or sales of military-style combat rifles to the general public and, as a matter of fact, sales of many of these weapons were banned federally by provisions of the 1994 Crime Bill. (Several states had already enacted bans on the ownership of these kinds of firearms.) Just as the small, cheap Saturday Night Special once was thought to be the "weapon of choice" for criminals (but turned out not to be), assault weapons are now commonly said to be the weapons of choice for drug dealers, youth gangs, and juvenile offenders of the sort studied here. There is practically no systematic evidence to support such an assertion. The fraction of guns confiscated from criminals by police that could be called assault weapons, even using liberal definitions, is not more than 1 or 2 percent (Kleck 1991:73).

For all the attention these assault weapons have received, it is worth stressing that, whether a matter of accessibility or preference, the most likely owned gun of either sample was a hand weapon (automatic or not) of at least .357 caliber. This is not to say they are uninterested in military-style equipment; more than one-third possessed a military-style assault rifle at the time of their incarceration. Still, these are highly specialized weapons that are generally ill suited for the day-to-day business of urban thuggery (or for protecting oneself against that thuggery). Outfitted with high-capacity magazines or clips, these weapons are bulky, relatively hard to handle, and impossible to conceal, and it would be a rare circumstance indeed that would require the firepower such weapons represent. For most offensive *and* defensive purposes, hand weapons are much better suited and, indeed, are far more commonly owned in both of our samples, as among the gun-owning public at large.

The recurrent emphasis in policy circles on specific *types* of guns (whether today's emphasis on military-style guns or the earlier emphasis on small, cheap handguns) is generally misplaced (Kleck 1991:Ch. 3). There may well be good reasons to restrict the availability of certain types of guns, but the attention now being given to military-style weapons illustrates what Kleck has called "searching for 'bad' guns," the persistent hope among gun control advocates that if we can just find a way to ban "bad guns" and leave "good guns" alone, we will reduce the level of crime and violence but not infringe on the rights of legitimate gun owners. Yet, since the "goodness" or "badness" of a gun surely inheres in the motivations and intentions of its user, not in the features of the gun itself, this approach, although commonly urged, is likely to be unproductive.

Turning from the issue of gun type to motivation, perhaps the most striking feature of our findings on juveniles' gun ownership is the *quality* of the firearms they possess. Theirs are not lesser weapons, Saturday Night Specials, homemade zip guns, or anything of the sort. Rather, they are mostly well made, easy to shoot, accurate, reliable firearms with considerable firepower. Many of the incarcerated juvenile felons we surveyed were as well armed as the police. Given the apparently pervasive atmosphere of violence and desperation (certainly given the *perception* of such an atmosphere by our respondents), the preference for high-quality, high-firepower small arms hardly comes as a surprise. Whether the intention is to protect what one has or to take by force what one wants, success depends on being adequately armed. The inner logic of an "arms race" seems altogether too apt. No street criminal (whether juvenile or adult) would willingly carry anything other than the best small arms he could lay hands on; neither would anyone seeking protection from those criminals. Given the evidently heavy flow of firearms of all sorts through the neighborhoods in question, the natural process of selection obviously favors large, well-made, highly lethal guns among both perpetrators and their possible victims, which is to say, among nearly everybody.[1]

The national alarm over youth and violence has been accompanied by insistent demands for "tough," "new" gun control legislation of one or another sort. We think there is probably some merit in increasing criminal penalties for the unlawful transfer of firearms to juveniles; if nothing else, this would give the police and the courts an extra plea-bargaining chip. But it is a sobering lesson that most of the methods used by juveniles to obtain guns already are against the law. Consider: It is already illegal for juveniles to purchase handguns through normal retail channels, pawnshops included. Likewise, it is already illegal to cross state lines to obtain guns. Theft of guns from homes, cars, and shipments is against the law; transferring or selling stolen property is also illegal. Transferring a firearm to a person with a criminal record is against the law. Possession of guns by persons with histories of alcohol or drug abuse is against the law. Street sources and friends who deal firearms to or make proxy purchases for juveniles are surely contributing to the delinquency of minors and are probably in violation of other laws as well.

Likewise, nearly everything juveniles do with their guns is already against the law. Unlicensed carrying of firearms is illegal everywhere; discharging firearms within city limits is illegal almost everywhere; bringing a gun onto school property is unlawful in most jurisdictions; assaults, robbery, murder, and other acts of violence are unlawful in every jurisdiction. Since we are not deterring juveniles from engaging in these behaviors in the first place, it is doubtful that increased threats regarding procurement of the tools to engage in the behaviors will accomplish much. The problem, it seems, is not that the appropriate laws do not exist. The problem instead is that the laws that do exist either are not or cannot be enforced due to the enormity of the problem and the lack of sufficient resources, and that the persons who are involved in firearms transactions with juveniles clearly are not concerned in the least with the legality of the transaction.

Informal commerce in small arms involving purchases, swaps, and trades among private parties is inherently difficult or impossible to regulate, is heavily exploited by juveniles as well as adults to obtain guns, and successfully subverts the legal apparatus we have erected to prevent guns from falling into the wrong hands (that is, controls imposed at the point of retail purchase). That much of the illicit commerce involves informal buys, swaps, and trades poses strict and obvious limits on the effectiveness of gun controls enacted at the point of retail sale, for example, the recently enacted Brady Law, which establishes a national five-day waiting period for handgun purchases. Since most "bad guys," adult and juvenile, do not obtain guns through normal retail channels, a five-day waiting period will not affect their firearms acquisitions. So far as juveniles specifically are concerned, retail sale of handguns is already illegal for persons under the age of twenty-one and retail sale of rifles and shotguns illegal for persons under age eighteen.

If retail sales are not the source of firearms for juveniles, then the illegal gun supply merits attention. It is fairly obvious that theft is the ultimate (if not proximate) source of many or most of the firearms that now circulate in the informal street market; otherwise, prices presumably would be higher. Theft erodes the distinction between legitimate and illegitimate firearms (or between "right hands" and "wrong hands"), since any firearm that can be legally possessed by a legitimate owner can be stolen from that owner and thus enter the illicit street commerce in guns. We feel there is merit in a national campaign to encourage responsible firearm ownership and to persuade legitimate firearm owners to store their weapons in such a way as to discourage theft. However, so long as guns are available to *anyone*, they will also be available to any *juvenile* or any *felon* with the means and motives to steal one or to exploit the informal network of family and friends to obtain a gun stolen by someone else. Surveys dating to the 1950s confirm that half the households in the United States possess one or more guns, and so on the average, a gun is available to be stolen in every second home.[2]

Seeing little hope in deterring juveniles from stealing legitimately owned guns, some gun control advocates reason that if guns were generally more difficult to obtain by the public at large, then there would be fewer guns available to steal. This in turn would reduce the number of guns circulating in the street market and thus decrease the number that fall into the "wrong hands." It seems to us that the "restricted-market" model is an example of reasoning from a correlation to a cause in exactly the wrong direction. If there were many fewer guns available to steal from the general gun-owning public, the street market in guns would not magically disappear; rather, more organized street sources would obtain the requisite supply of firearms from other sources. The general lack of organized supply at the moment is mostly a function of the relatively low profit associated with selling guns to juveniles: the supply is just too great. Even if we could halt the entire domestic production of firearms, which is very unlikely, and also confiscate the larger share of the two hundred million or so firearms currently in circulation in the United States (Wright et al. 1983; Kleck 1991), even less likely, there is little we could do to prevent the manufacture of firearms elsewhere in the world or their illegal importation into this country. If it is possible to organize a system of commerce to bring hundreds of tons of cocaine from Colombia and get it into the hands of people on the streets of our cities, it is certainly possible to organize a system that will bring hundreds of tons of small arms from Israel or Switzerland or the Czech Republic or Brazil and supply a street market in firearms as well.

We have no evidence in the present study to suggest that an international illicit market in small arms already exists (at least not as a supplier to our kind of respondent). That is because theft is a *convenient* way to obtain firearms for street sale in the current regulatory and gun ownership environment. It does not follow that if we could eliminate that convenience by reducing household stockpiles, we would therefore shut down the street market entirely. More generally, if a demand for some commodity exists, be it guns, drugs, pornography, or whatever, then satisfying that demand will be a profitable enterprise. The commodity will be supplied through an illegal network of smuggling and distribution if no other market mechanism is available. Bans on otherwise desired commodities will sometimes affect their price but generally not their availability to anyone willing to pay the price. And if, as we have suggested, guns may now be a bargain at any price (standing as the last line of defense against predation, intimidation, or death), then efforts to deal with the violence problem through restrictions on the potential supply of firearms are bound not to be very effective. A juvenile who "must have a gun" now can easily steal enough money to purchase one on the street; that same juvenile likely will work somewhat harder to steal more money to obtain the more expensive weapon.

Recognizing that prohibition of retail gun sales to juveniles has generally not prevented young people from arming themselves, many jurisdictions are currently contemplating the passage of legislation that would make it illegal for juveniles even to possess guns. Presumably, the point of such legislation is to give the police a reason to arrest a young person found to be carrying a gun. But unlicensed carrying of guns is already illegal for juveniles and adults alike; more generally, it is hard to believe that the police could not find a legitimate reason to arrest virtually any juvenile they thought to be carrying a gun in the absence of a legal prohibition against juvenile firearms possession. Thus it is difficult to see the exact point of this sort of legislation. As in many other cases involving "gun control," the point seems more symbolic than practical; the intent is more to strike a posture of concern about the problem of juvenile violence than to provide police or the courts with legislative tools necessary to do their job.

Disrupting the Illegal Gun Market

Assuming that little can be done to alter the number of guns circulating in this country, some have suggested harassing the sellers of guns to the point that it is just too difficult to do business profitably. Reiss and Roth (1993), for example, argue for centralized and street-level tactics to disrupt illegal gun sales, like those now used to intervene in illegal drug markets. Such tactics might include

> buy-bust operations, high-priority investigation and prosecution of alleged unregulated gun dealers, the development of minors arrested in possession of guns as informants against gun sources, phony fencing operations for stolen guns, high priority investigations and prosecutions of burglaries and robberies in which guns are stolen, and high mandatory minimum sentences for those who steal or illegally sell guns. (p. 280)

On the one hand, it is hard to imagine a "war on guns" that borrows tactics from a fairly obviously failed "war on drugs" (Inciardi 1992). On the other, according to researcher David M. Kennedy (1994), a disruption experiment in Tampa, Florida, seems to have had a noticeable impact on drug dealing in that city. A heavy and directed police presence around known dealing sites forced drug dealers to move around more than they wished. "Reverse stings" (in which buyers were arrested by police posing as dealers) frightened potential customers. Dealers' drug stashes were located and seized. Dealers' places of business (abandoned houses, shops, etc.) were closed or torn down. Local ordinances were employed to clear crowds from known trafficking sites. The power of such harassment lay in its multiple attacks on the free functioning of the drug market. In Kennedy's estimation, six months of concentrated disruption virtually eliminated dealers from public activity.

Can such tactics be applied to the suppliers of guns on the illegal market? Kennedy sees possible parallels. By way of illustration, he suggests that police could cultivate informants who could identify persons with stockpiles of guns and could offer juveniles caught with guns plea bargains based on giving up their suppliers. They could press for state laws making those who sell guns to juveniles jointly liable for crimes committed with those guns. They could mount reverse sting operations and coordinate drug and firearm offensives so that drug dealers who also profit from gun sales would view the police attention to guns as bad for the drug business. Stores, bars, and other businesses that front for those selling guns to juveniles could be shut down through civil or licensing proceedings. In short, there seem to be a number of means by which to make the sale of firearms to juveniles more difficult and less profitable.

Until such tactics are evaluated experimentally, their potency is uncertain. Undoubtedly, they will have *some* positive effect. Overall, though, there are some serious issues to be addressed. First, the cost of prolonged concentration of police resources to the level of harassment in question may be prohibitive for many communities. Second, Kennedy argues that the goal of harassment of drug dealers is the absence of public drug dealing, and thus the public perception of community disorder. Clearly, highly visible, public gun transactions can and should be discouraged. But most illegal gun transactions are not so blatant; most citizens have observed drugs being sold at one time or another, but few have seen firearms peddled. While the public feels better when drug transactions are driven underground, the issue regarding guns is not transactions but uses of guns. Harassment of gun dealers may disrupt sales, but will they influence gun use patterns?

Third and related, though juveniles appear interested in new and better guns, the fact remains that a given juvenile only needs *one* firearm. Here the interest in acquiring firearms differs from that associated with acquiring drugs. Drugs disappear when used, and stocks must be replenished. Guns need only be reloaded.[3] In the final analysis, disruption of the gun market likely will have two results: guns will cost more but interested youth will raise the funds to make the one purchase they see as necessary; they will then hold onto that one gun for a longer period before "trading up." The accuracy of this gaze into the crystal ball, of course, is as open to refutation as are any of the potential disruption possibilities Kennedy suggests.

Drugs and Guns

If controlling guns and disrupting gun sales is not likely to reduce firearm-related violence, where then do we turn? As we have suggested, the key to understanding the problem of juveniles and guns lies not in the trigger that is being pulled but in the juvenile's perceived need and evident willingness to pull that trigger. In short, we need to explore the juvenile's motivation for carrying and using firearms if we are to devise strategies to reduce such activities.

Much has been made in the media of the role that drugs play in gun-related violence among juveniles. Our findings do not belie these understandings, but they do suggest greater complexity to the relationships than is ordinarily assumed. We note, first, that it is not wholly clear that drug activity drives gun activity today as it may have some years ago. Street gang homicide in Chicago, for example, has had relatively little to do with drugs in recent years (Block and Block 1993; see also Klein, Maxson, and Cunningham. 1991). We believe that ten years ago the average urban juvenile with a gun likely had some connection to drug trafficking. Picture such youths as lying at the core of a series of concentric circles. Those in the circle immediately adjacent to the core, only marginally involved in drugs, nonetheless felt endangered by the youth at the core and responded by carrying guns. Those in the next ring then were threatened and followed suit. Ultimately, the problem rippled to urban areas (and, if our data concerning suburban gun use are generalizable, beyond urban areas) once considered immune to it. And with that spread came a shift in the mean use of a gun. The norm no longer appears drug related, but protection or dispute related.

Second, it is abundantly clear that to the extent drug use of *any* kind increases, so also do criminal behavior, gun possession, and gun use. Drug *dealing* at any level is also linked to higher levels of crime and gun-related activity. Nonetheless, the majority of both inmate and student respondents did not use hard drugs and few who did used regularly (i.e., more than a few times a year). The popular image of inner-city youth and, especially, criminally involved inner-city youth as drug addicts one and all finds little support here. Substantial numbers of non-users among our respondents had committed serious crimes and had significant levels of gun-related activities.

Our interpretation of these findings is that drug activity is less a precipitant of crime and gun use than one crucial element in the new subculture of inner-city underclass youth. That is, the drug epidemic in the inner cities has certainly worsened the problems of crime and violence, but it is misleading to think that drugs per se are their ultimate or final cause (Wright and Devine 1994). The primal attraction of drugs is that they provide immediate gratification; they give a sense of euphoria or well-being *right now*. Arguments against using drugs—that one might *become* an addict or *eventually* destroy one's physical health—all require an orientation toward the future, a concern, in short, about tomorrow's consequences of today's behaviors. And this is precisely the sort of orientation, we argue below, that the structural conditions of the inner city have destroyed among many of its youth.

In this sense, drugs are not the cause of crime and violence so much as they are indicative or symptomatic of a more general unraveling of social norms, values, and expectations that otherwise constrain behavior. What has arisen in the inner city is a subculture where anything goes, a subculture that is essentially defined by estrangement from—indeed, hostility to—the norms and conventions of the larger society. That this subculture is rejected and even despised by the majority of inner-city residents does not exempt the majority from the need to live with and deal with its consequences.

When all is said and done, the drug epidemic has become a convenient scapegoat for many of the ills of the inner city. This, however, mistakes a symptom for a cause. Three-quarters of our juvenile inmates have fired a gun at someone. Most did *not* do so because they were high on drugs or because they were strung out and needed more drugs; most did so because they live in a moral universe that ascribes no particular value to a human life, that counsels no hesitance in pulling the trigger, that promotes immediate gratification for the very simple reason that tomorrow may never come. Inner-city juveniles (or more accurately put, that minority of inner-city juveniles whose anomic and antisocial behavior now defines the conditions of life in the cities) own and carry guns, use and deal drugs, and perpetrate crimes and violence all for the same reasons: because they have little or no discernible future to which they can aspire and therefore nothing much better to do.

Gangs and Guns

What has just been said about drugs and guns can also be said about gangs and guns. The public image linking youth gangs with urban violence is not wholly supported by our findings. On the one hand, youth who are involved in gang activities also show higher levels of gun possession and use; the more structured the gang involvement, the stronger these tendencies. Yet, one-third of our inmate respondents claimed no prior affiliation with a gang. Only 22 percent of the student sample were affiliated with a gang. Thus, judging from our findings, a sizable percentage of criminally active youth and a very large percentage of inner-city high school students have no gang involvements. Gun possession and usage is far more common than is gang membership.

Like drugs, the gang has become an all-purpose scapegoat for the afflictions of the inner city. As a form of social organization, gangs exist for some purpose and reason. In the context of the contemporary urban underclass, gangs exist because there is safety in numbers and because they provide some degree of organization and control in what are otherwise disorganized, out-of-control neighborhoods. In many cases, urban gangs have assumed the "social control" function that the customary agents of social control can no longer adequately provide. They also give estranged youth something meaningful to which to belong, a source of identity that is otherwise lacking. Gangs express the pathology of inner-city underclass life and the new urban culture of violence, but are the consequence of these developments more than the cause.

Urban Structure and Culture

It is probably true that every major U.S. city could make a substantial short-term dent in its crime and violence problems by incarcerating several hundred of its high-rate juvenile offenders; mandatory and severe sentencing is yet another commonly urged approach to the juvenile violence problem. But all else equal in terms of extant social environment, there will soon be several hundred new high-rate juvenile offenders to take their place. Shall we continue this process until we have incarcerated an entire class of the urban population?

There is a useful analogy to be drawn between the violence problem and the yellow fever problem that plagued many southern cities in the nineteenth century. The vector for the yellow fever infection was eventually found to be the mosquito; once that essential fact was learned, it became possible to control yellow fever by eradicating the conditions under which mosquitoes bred. No one suggested that the solution to yellow fever was to wander through the swamps of Louisiana removing the mouthparts of mosquitoes with little tweezers, so they could no longer bite people and thereby spread the infection. Guns, we suggest, are the "mouthparts" of our contemporary epidemic of violence; as such, "gun control" has no better chance of solving the violence problem than "proboscis control" had to solve the yellow fever problem.

Daniel Polsby (1994) offers a similarly useful analogy, in this instance between the population of violent offenders and the population of game animals such as deer. His essential insight is that the size of the herd is determined strictly by the carrying capacity of the habitat, not by annual efforts to cull it, for example, through hunting. Imprisoning violent juvenile offenders is very much like culling the herd; the measure will result in a short-term reduction in herd size but the herd will quickly breed back up to the carrying capacity limit. The opportunities and motivations to commit crime, and therefore the number of crimes that are committed, are features of the urban habitat. Over any sufficiently long period, therefore, the number of offenders and offenses will not be affected by the rate of incarceration. In the absence of attention to the defining features of the urban habitat, proposals to control juvenile crime through increased incarceration are doomed.

To this point, our search for policy to reduce gun-related violence has focused on attempts to keep firearms out of the hands of juveniles. We see little hope in this vein. As well, we have examined the presence of drug and gang activities as central features of the violent social environment and have found them implicated in but not wholly explicative of urban violence. Strictly speaking, the nature of our data on juveniles and guns permits exploration of little else. However, two findings surely point toward contemporary urban structure and culture as the source of gun-related activity among youth and as the necessary target of change in the level of that activity. First, there are simply too many juveniles in possession of and carrying guns to indicate that the cause and cure lie with individual carriers or even with social phenomena like gangs and drugs. Second, our findings indicate dramatically that, for the majority of inner-city youth, inmates and students alike, self-protection in a hostile, violent, and dangerous world is the chief reason to own and carry guns. By default, these findings indicate the need to reduce the *demand* for guns, which implies addressing the inner-city problems (beyond drugs and gangs) for which guns have become the perceived solution.

It is erroneous to depict every poor neighborhood in every large city as a killing field or to suggest that all residents of the inner city now go about their daily business armed. At the same time, it is also a mistake to understate the levels of violence and fear of violence that now pervade inner-city life. In the past few years, homicide rates in nearly every major city have reached record highs. Arrests for drug offenses have swollen jail and prison populations beyond capacity; most cities of which we are aware find themselves plagued by increasingly violent youth gangs. Surveys of young children in inner cities report astonishingly high percentages who say they have seen someone shot or seen a dead body in the streets. In circumstances such as these, possession of a firearm provides a necessary if otherwise undesirable edge against the uncertainty of police protection and the daily threat of intimidation or victimization.

The pervasive atmosphere of violence extends from the streets into the schools. Male and female respondents to our survey alike viewed their schools as relatively violent places. Fourteen percent of the males and 15 percent of the females described themselves as scared in school most of the time. Just under 50 percent of each group knew schoolmates at whom shots had been fired. The level of violent victimization among the students was exceptionally high. Twenty percent of the males and 6 percent of the females had been shot at in or on the way to or from school. Ten percent of the males and 7 percent of the females had been stabbed. Both reacting to and promoting this violence, 3 percent of the males and 1 percent of the females carry a gun to school all or most of the time.

The perception that so many people are armed presumably combines with the reality of frequent victimization and with routine transit through precarious places (including schools) and involvement in dangerous activities (such as drug deals, gang ventures, and crimes) to create what amounts to a siege mentality among individuals and a subculture of fear for inner-city youth in the aggregate. More than two-thirds of the inmates we surveyed, for example, said they had fired guns in self-defense. Among the activities that increase the likelihood of gun possession and use are gun dealing and drug dealing (nearly half of the inmates had dealt guns, more than 80 percent had dealt drugs). Gun and drug dealers are considerably more likely to engage in serious criminal activity as well. In general, the more dangerous the environment and activities of juveniles, the more likely they are to own and carry firearms.

The apparent implication of these findings is that our juveniles are strongly, not weakly, motivated to own and carry guns; these behaviors appear, in our findings at least, to be largely utilitarian reactions to life in neighborhoods ruled more and more by predation, that is, neighborhoods where the police can*not* be counted on to protect life and property. Surely, when people have concluded that their very ability to survive depends on the protection and power that having a gun affords, then arguments against owning and carrying guns become unpersuasive. That many of our juveniles seek protection from one another does not diminish the point; if the issue is indeed survival, then weapons are a bargain at nearly any price.

It is not necessary to review here *all* the various social, economic, and structural conditions that have created this emergent underclass culture. In brief, the national poverty rate has been generally increasing since about 1980, and so the sheer number of the poor has increased, especially in the central cities. Even more troubling, the rate of *chronic* poverty has increased (Devine, Plunkett, and Wright 1992). At the same time, the poverty of the poor has deepened as the gap between affluence and poverty has widened; the proportion of total national income going to the poorest quintile now stands at the lowest point in the twentieth century. Simultaneously, nearly all central cities have been losing population for the past two decades as more affluent middle-class families, black and white, leave for the suburban fringe. The net result of these economic and demographic developments is an increasing concentration of increasingly poor people in inner-city areas and a substantially reduced tax base to provide the revenues required to respond to the increasingly deeper needs of the population that remains. The neighborhoods are deteriorating, infested with dealers, addicts, criminals, and other vermin, both human and otherwise (Skogan 1990). City services range from pathetic to nonexistent; no one tends to public spaces or collects the trash and litter. Many areas are essentially unpoliced, their perimeters defined more or less officially as the boundaries of free-fire zones within which anything goes.

Other developments have exacerbated the resulting problems. Critically, the proportion of young people among the inner-city poor has also sharply increased (Wilson 1987:36–37). Public schools are generally in disarray, dropout rates are high and increasing, joblessness among young central city nonwhite males now routinely exceeds 40 or 50 percent, and vast numbers of entry-level manufacturing jobs have exited the urban areas for the suburbs or abroad (Kasarda 1985). The consequence is an increasingly large cohort of impoverished young people without adequate educations and with little or no prospects for decent jobs—a cohort to whom, in essence, conventional routes of upward mobility have been closed off. Many of these youth have a much better chance of going to prison than going to college, a better chance of becoming homeless or addicted than of becoming stably employed.

Within African-American communities, the exodus of successful, upwardly mobile persons from the inner city has left the young with fewer and fewer role models; the steady deterioration of the inner-city economic structure has created joblessness and underemployment on a vast scale; the decline of indigenous community organizations such as black churches and black-owned businesses has further reduced the presence of successful lives to emulate and respect. "Thus, in such neighborhoods the chances are overwhelming that children will seldom interact on a sustained basis with people who are employed or with families that have a steady breadwinner" (Wilson 1987:57). The role models that remain are the drug dealers, pimps, and thugs who play by a different set of rules and, within the context, prove relatively successful at it.

Lacking an attainable future, or at least the belief in one, and absent models of deferred gratification and conventional success, it is all too easy to see how life can quickly become a quest for the immediate gratification of present impulses, a moment-to-moment existence where weighing the consequences of today's behavior against their future implications is largely pointless. Given, too, a larger culture that increasingly defines personal worth in terms of one's ability to consume, and a social and economic situation wherein one's ability to consume often depends on being able to take what one wants, the sense of personal merit or self-esteem easily comes to imply being stronger, meaner, and better armed than others.

Much is written these days about "empowerment" as the nearly universal solution to the problems of the disenfranchised. The point is well taken in that the powerless are forever at the mercy of others. And certainly, poor urban minority youth must be counted as among the most disadvantaged and least powerful groups in American society. Imagine, then, the empowerment that results when inner-city teenagers wrap their fingers around firearms. In that act, they suddenly become people to be feared, whose wishes must be respected, whose bidding must be done. With so much of the day-to-day reality of existence clearly beyond their control, they can at least decide where to point the gun and when to pull the trigger. It is very clearly agency of a high order.

To avoid misunderstanding, it must be stressed that underclass culture is *not* a majority culture among the inner-city poor, not even among the poor inner-city youth represented (for example) by our high school respondents. It should go without saying that the majority of poor people in the inner cities remain hard-working, law-abiding people. The concern, rather, is that the culture of the underclass has become (or is becoming) the *defining* aspect of the inner city, such that even those who reject it in entirety must nonetheless organize their lives around the reality it represents. In exactly this sense, Wilson (1987:38; see also Rose and McClain 1990) posits a "critical mass" of disaffected and hostile youth that, once exceeded, can literally explode into a "self-sustaining chain reaction" of crime, violence, addiction, and predation, a relatively small group whose influence on the life of the inner city is all out of proportion to its actual numbers.

Against this backdrop, what do our findings and interpretations suggest about the ongoing policy debate concerning juveniles and violence? Many of the terms of debate—drugs, gangs, even guns themselves—prove to be essentially epiphenomenal. They provide a method of restating the problem but do not and cannot suggest a solution. Guns, drugs, gangs, crime, and violence are all expressions of a pervasive alienation of certain inner-city youth from the conventions of larger society. We can seek to impose our will, pass new legislation to outlaw that of which we disapprove, and insist on harsher punishments for those who defy our rules. Ultimately, however, convincing inner-city juveniles (or adults) not to own, carry, and use guns requires convincing them that they can survive in their neighborhoods without being armed, that they can come and go in peace, that their unarmed condition will not cause them to be victimized, intimidated, or slain. Until we attend to the conditions that promote insecurity and fear and that breed hostility, estrangement, futility, and hopelessness, the perception that firearms are necessary to survival in the inner city will endure.

Notes

1.   In this vein consider the description of firearms given by one Los Angeles central city youth to another who just got out of prison: "[L]et me explain what fullies do. They don't blow you up, they don't shoot you, they *spray* you. . . . Sprays are permanent. They ain't no joke. We got shit that shoots seventy-five times. . . . The latest things out are fullies, body armor, and pagers. Offense, defense, and communication. . . . I got a Glock model seventeen that shoots eighteen times. It's a hand strap. Bro, this is the real world" (Scott 1993:366–67).

2.   It should not be assumed that guns owned by adults and stored in homes and cars were purchased legally, i.e., not "hot," on the black market. In short, juvenile demand may be only one element driving an illegal gun market; the problem of illegal access to guns may involve more citizens of more ages than we think.

3.   There is considerable attention now being given to the issue of control of ammunition supplies as a form of gun control (see Moynihan 1993). It is doubtful that such a tactic will produce large-scale results. Ammunition is even easier to produce and export into the United States than are guns. For that matter, black market demands for ammunition likely will foster the creation of domestic cottage industries to produce bullets.

REFERENCES

Akers, R. 1992. *Drugs, Alcohol, and Society*. Belmont, CA: Wadsworth.

Akers, R., J. Massey, W. Clarke, and R. Lauer. 1983. "Are Self-Reports of Adolescent Deviance Valid?" *Social Forces* 62:234–51.

Allen-Hagen, B. and M. Sickmund. 1993. *Juveniles and Violence: Juvenile Offending and Victimization*. OJJDP Fact Sheet. Washington, DC: U.S. Department of Justice.

Altschuler, D. and P. Brounstein. 1991. "Patterns of Drug Use, Drug Trafficking and Other Delinquency Among Inner City Adolescent Males in Washington, DC." *Criminology* 29:589–621.

Anderson, A., A. Basilevsky, and D. Hum. 1983. "Missing Data: A Review of the Literature." Pp. 415–94 in *Handbook of Survey Research*, edited by P. Rossi, J. Wright, and A. Anderson. New York: Academic Press.

Anglin, M. D. and G. Speckart. 1986. "Narcotics Use, Property Crime, and Dealing: Structural Dynamics Across the Addiction Career." *Journal of Quantitative Criminology* 2:355–75.

Asmussen, K. J. 1992. "Weapon Possession in Public High Schools." *School Safety* (Fall):28–30.

Auletta, K. 1983. *The Underclass*. New York: Viking.

Bastion, L. D. and B. M. Taylor. 1991. *School Crime: A National Crime Victimization Survey Report*. Washington, DC: Department of Justice.

Bayh, B. 1975. *Our Nation's Schools—A Report Card: "A" in School Violence and Vandalism*. Washington, DC: United States Senate, Committee on the Judiciary.

Beck, A., S. Kline, and L. Greenfeld. 1988. *Survey of Youth in Custody, 1987*. Washington, DC: Bureau of Justice Statistics.

Block, C. and R. Block. 1993. *Street Gang Crime in Chicago*. Washington, DC: U.S. Department of Justice.

Bluestone, B. and B. Harrison. 1982. *The Deindustrialization of America: Plant Closings, Community Abandonment, and the Dismantling of Basic Industry*. New York: Basic Books.

Blumstein, A., D. Farrington, and S. Moitra. 1985. "Delinquency Careers: Innocents, Desisters, and Persisters." Pp. 187–219 in *Crime and Justice: An Annual Review of Research, Vol. 6,* edited by M. Tonry and M. Morris. Chicago: University of Chicago Press.

Callahan, C. and F. Rivara. 1992. "Urban High School Youth and Handguns." *Journal of the American Medical Association* 267:3038–42.

Callahan, C., F. Rivara, and J. Farrow. 1993. "Youth in Detention and Handguns." *Journal of Adolescent Health* 14:350–55.

Campbell, A. 1990. "Female Participation in Gangs." Pp. 163–82 in *Gangs in America,* edited by C. Ronald Huff. Newbury Park, CA: Sage.

Cartwright, D., K. Howard, and N. Reuterman. 1970. "Multivariate Analysis of Gang Delinquency: II. Structural and Dynamic Properties of Gangs." *Multivariate Behavioral Research* 5:303–23.

Cernkovich, S., P. Giordano, and M. Pugh. 1985. "Chronic Offenders: The Missing Cases in Self-Report Delinquency Research." *Journal of Criminal Law and Criminology* 76:705–32.

Chaiken, J. M. and M. R. Chaiken. 1982. *Varieties of Criminal Behavior.* Santa Monica, CA: Rand.

Chaiken, J. M. and M. R. Chaiken. 1990. "Drugs and Predatory Crime." Pp. 203–39 in *Drugs and Crime,* edited by M. Tonry and J. Q. Wilson. Chicago: University of Chicago Press.

Chaiken, M. R. and B. D. Johnson. 1988. "Characteristics of Different Types of Drug-Involved Offenders." *Issues and Practices.* Washington, DC: National Institute of Justice.

Chicago Tribune. 1992. "Schools Confront Gun Threat." 7 December.

Chin, K. 1990. *Chinese Subculture and Criminality: Non-Traditional Crime Groups in America.* Westport, CT: Greenwood.

Christoffel, K. K. 1992. "Pediatric Firearm Injuries: Time to Target a Growing Population." *Pediatric Annals* 21:430–36.

Clark, J. and L. Tifft. 1966. "Polygraph and Interview Validation of Self-Reported Delinquent Behavior." *American Sociological Review* 31:516–23.

Clogg, C. 1981. "New Developments in Latent Structure Analysis." Pp. 214–80 in *Factor Analysis and Measurement in Sociological Research,* edited by David J. Jackson and Edgar F. Borgotta. Beverly Hills, CA: Sage.

Collison, B., S. Bowden, M. Patterson, et al. 1987. "After the Shooting Stops." *Journal of Counseling and Development* 65:389–90.

Conklin, J. 1972. *Robbery and the Criminal Justice System.* Philadelphia: Lippincott.

Cook, P. 1976. "A Strategic Choice Analysis of Robbery." Pp. 173–87 in *Sample Surveys of the Victims of Crime,* edited by W. Skogan. Cambridge, MA: Ballinger.

Cook, P. 1980. "Reducing Injury and Death Rates in Robbery." *Policy Analysis* 6:21–45.

Cooper, B. M. 1987. "Motor City Breakdown." *Village Voice* 1:23–35.

Curry, G. D. and I. A. Spergel. 1988. "Gang Homicide, Delinquency and Community." *Criminology* 26:381–405.

David R. and J. Siegenthaler. 1985. "Violence in the Schools." Pp. 678–90 in *Violence: Perspectives on Murder and Aggression*. Washington, DC: Congressional Information Service.

Devine, J. and J. Wright. 1993. *The Greatest of Evils*. Hawthorne, NY: Aldine de Gruyter.

Devine, J., M. Plunkett, and J. Wright. 1992. "The Chronicity of Poverty." *Social Forces* 70:787–812.

Duke, D. and C. Perry. 1979. "What Happened to the High School Discipline Crisis?" *Urban Education* 2:192–204.

Elliott, D. and S. Ageton. 1980. "Reconciling Differences in Estimates of Delinquency." *American Sociological Review* 45:95–110.

Elliott, D., D. Huizinga, and S. Menard. 1989. *Multiple Problem Youth: Delinquency, Drugs, and Mental Health*. New York: Springer-Verlag.

Elliott, D. and H. Voss. 1974. *Delinquency and Dropout*. Lexington, MA: Lexington.

Eskin, L. 1989. "An All-American Teen's Descent Into a Life of Drugs and Crime". *Scholastic Update* 122:7.

Fagan, J. 1989. "The Social Organization of Drug Use and Drug Dealing among Urban Gangs." *Criminology* 27:633–69.

Fagan, J. 1990. "Social Processes of Delinquency and Drug Use among Urban Gangs." Pp. 183–219 in *Gangs in America*, edited by C. R. Huff. Newbury Park, CA: Sage.

Fagan, J. 1992. "Drug Selling and Illicit Incidents in Distressed Neighborhoods." Pp. 99–146 in *Drugs, Crime, and Social Isolation*, edited by A. Harrell and G. Peterson. Washington, DC: Urban Institute Press.

Fagan, J. and K. Chin. 1990. "Violence as Regulation and Social Control in the Distribution of Crack." In *Drugs and Violence*, edited by M. de la Rosa, E. Lambert, and B. Gropper. Rockville, MD: National Institute on Drug Abuse.

Fagan, J., E. Piper, and Y. Cheng. 1987. "Contributions of Victimization to Delinquency in Inner Cities." *Journal of Criminal Law and Criminology* 78:586–613.

Fagan, J., E. Piper, and M. Moore. 1986. "Violent Delinquents and Urban Youths." *Criminology* 23:439–66.

Fagan, J. and J. Weis. 1990. *Drug Use and Delinquency Among Inner City Youth*. New York: Springer-Verlag.

Farrington, D. 1973. "Self Reports of Deviant Behavior: Predictive and Stable?" *Journal of Crime and Criminology* 64:99–110.

Federal Bureau of Investigation. 1993. *Uniform Crime Reports, 1992*. Washington, DC: U.S. Government Printing Office.

Felson, M. 1987. "Routine Activities and Crime Prevention in the Developing Metropolis." *Criminology* 25:911–31.

Felson, M. 1994. *Crime and Everyday Life*. Thousand Oaks, CA: Pine Forge.

Fingerhut, L. 1993. "Firearm Mortality Among Children, Youth, and Young Adults 1–34 Years of Age, Trends, and Current Status: United States, 1985–1990." National Center for Health Statistics. *Advance Data* 231(March 23).

Fingerhut, L. and J. Kleinman. 1990. "International and Interstate Comparisons of Homicide Among Young Males." *Journal of the American Medical Association* 263:3292–295.

Fingerhut, L., J. Kleinman, E. Godfrey, and H. Rosenberg. 1991. "Firearm Mortality Among Children, Youth, and Young Adults 1–34 Years of age, Trends and Current Status: United States, 1979–1988." *Monthly Vital Statistics Report, No. 11 (Supp.)*. Hyattsville, MD: National Center for Health Statistics.

Fitzpatrick, K. 1993. "Exposure to Violence and Presence of Depression Among Low-Income, African-American Youth." *Journal of Consulting and Clinical Psychology* 61:528–31.

Gentry, C. 1995. "Crime Control Through Drug Control." Pp. 477–93 in *Criminology: A Contemporary Handbook*, 2nd ed., edited by J. Sheley. Belmont, CA: Wadsworth.

Gladstein, J., E. Rusonis, and F. Heald. 1992. "A Comparison of Inner-City and Upper-Middle Class Youths' Exposure to Violence." *Journal of Adolescent Health* 13:275–80.

Goldstein, P. 1985. "The Drugs/Violence Issue: A Tripartite Conceptual Framework." *Journal of Drug Issues* 15:493–506.

Gottfredson, G. and D. Gottfredson. 1985. *Victimization in Schools*. New York: Plenum.

Gottfredson, M. and T. Hirschi. 1990. *A General Theory of Crime*. Stanford, CA: Stanford University Press.

Greenwood, P. 1980. *Rand Research on Criminal Careers*. Santa Monica, CA: Rand.

Gurule, J. 1991. "OJP Initiative on Gangs: Drugs and Violence in America." National Institute of Justice Reports, No. 224, pp. 4–5. Washington, DC: National Institute of Justice.

Hackett, G., R. Sandza, F. Gibney, and R. Gareiss. 1988. "Kids: Deadly Force." *Newsweek* (January 11):18–19.

Hagedorn, J. M. 1988. *People and Folks: Gangs, Crime and the Underclass in a Rustbelt City.* Chicago: Lake View.

Hardt, R. and S. Peterson-Hardt. 1977. "On Determining the Quality of the Delinquency Self-Report Method." *Journal of Research in Crime and Delinquency* 14:247–61.

Harrington, M. 1984. *The New American Poverty*. New York: Holt, Rinehart and Winston.

Harrington-Lueker, D. 1989. "Protecting Schools from Outside Violence." *Education Digest* 55:46–9.

Hellman, D. and S. Beaton. 1986. "The Pattern of Violence in Urban Public Schools: The Influence of School and Community." *Journal of Research in Crime and Delinquency* 23:102–7.

Hindelang, M. J., T. Hirschi, and J. G. Weis. 1981. *Measuring Delinquency*. Beverly Hills, CA: Sage.

Hirschi, T. 1969. *Causes of Delinquency*. Berkeley, CA: University of California Press.

Horney, J. and I. Marshall. 1992. "An Empirical Comparison of Two Self-Report Methods for Measuring Lambda." *Journal of Research in Crime and Delinquency* 29:102–21.

Horowitz, R. 1983. *Honor and the American Dream*. New Brunswick, NJ: Rutgers University Press.

Huizinga, D. and D. Elliott. 1986. "Reassessing the Reliability and Validity of Self-Report Delinquency Measures." *Journal of Quantitative Criminology* 2:293–327.

Inciardi, J. 1992. *The War on Drugs II*. Mountain View, CA: Mayfield.

Jackson, P. and C. Rudman. 1993. "Moral Panic and the Response to Gangs in California." Pp. 257–75 in *Gangs*, edited by S. Cummings and D. Monti . Albany: SUNY Press.

Jackson, R. and W. McBride. 1985. *Understanding Street Gangs*. Costa Mesa, CA: Custom.

Jankowski, M. S. 1991. *Islands in the Street: Gangs and American Urban Society*. Berkeley: University of California Press.

Jansyn, L. 1966. "Solidarity and Delinquency in a Street Corner Group." *American Sociological Review* 31:600–14.

Jencks, C. and P. Peterson. 1991. *The Urban Underclass*. Washington, DC: Brookings.

Jensen, G. and D. Brownfield. 1986. "Gender, Lifestyles, and Victimization: Beyond Routine Activity Theory." *Violence and Victims* 1:85–99.

Jensen, G. and D. Rojek. 1980. *Delinquency: A Sociological View*. Lexington, MA: Heath.

Johnson, B. D., T. Williams, K. A. Dei, and H. Sanabria. 1990. "Drug Abuse in the Inner City: Impact on Hard-Drug Users and the Community." Pp. 9–67 in *Drugs and Crime*, edited by M. Tonry and J. Q. Wilson. Chicago: University of Chicago Press.

Kasarda, J. 1985. "Urban Change and Minority Opportunities." Pp. 33–67 in *The New Urban Reality*, edited by P. Peterson. Washington, DC: Brookings.

Kennedy, D. 1994. "Can We Keep Guns Away from Kids." *American Prospect* 18:74–80.

Kleck, G. 1991. *Point Blank: Guns and Violence in America*. Hawthorne, New York: Aldine de Gruyter.

Kleck, G. 1993. "The Incidence of Gun Violence among Young People." *Public Perspective* (September/October): 3–6.

Kleiman M. and K. Smith. 1990. "State and Local Drug Enforcement: In Search of a Strategy." Pp. 69–108 in *Drugs and Crime*, edited by M. Tonry and J. Wilson. Chicago: University of Chicago Press.

Klein, M. 1984. "Offence Specialization and Versatility among Juveniles." *British Journal of Criminology* 24:185–94.

Klein, M., M. Gordon, and C. Maxson. 1986. "The Impact of Police Investigations on Police-Related Rates of Gang and Nongang Homicides." *Criminology* 24:489–512.

Klein, M. and C. Maxson. 1989. "Street Gang Violence." Pp. 198–234 in *Violent Crime, Violent Criminals*, edited by N. Warner and M. Wolfgang. Newbury Park, CA: Sage.

Klein, M., C. Maxson, and L. Cunningham. 1991. "'Crack,' Street Gangs, and Violence." *Criminology* 29:623–50.

Lauritsen, J., J. Laub, and R. Sampson. 1992. "Conventional and Delinquent Activities: Implications for the Prevention of Violent Victimization among Adolescents." *Violence and Victims* 7:91–108.

Lauritsen, J., R. Sampson, and J. Laub. 1991. "The Link between Offending and Victimization among Adolescents." *Criminology* 29:265–91.

Lazarsfeld, P. and N. Henry. 1968. *Latent Structure Analysis*. Boston: Houghton Mifflin.

Leslie, C. 1988. "Pencils, Papers, and Guns: Dade County Children Learn the ABCs of Firearms." *Newsweek* (December 5):92.

Lizotte, A., J. Tesoriero, T. Thornberry, and M. Krohn. 1994. "Patterns of Adolescent Firearms Ownership and Use." *Justice Quarterly* 11: 51–73.

Maxson, C. L., Gordon, M. A., and M. W. Klein. 1985. "Differences Between Gang and Nongang Homicides." *Criminology* 23:209–22.

Maxson, C. L. and M. W. Klein. 1990. "Street Gang Violence: Twice as Great or Half as Great?" Pp. 71–100 in *Gangs in America*, edited by C. R. Huff. Newbury Park, CA: Sage.

McDermott, M. J. 1983. "Crime in the School and in the Community." *Crime and Delinquency* 29:207–82.

McDonald, J. and R. Moffitt. 1980. "The Uses of Tobit Analysis." *Review of Economics and Statistics* 62:318–21.

McKinney, K. 1988. "Juvenile Gangs: Crime and Drug Trafficking." *Juvenile Justice Bulletin* (September). Washington, DC: Department of Justice.

Mieczkowski, T. 1986. "Geeking Up or Throwing Down: Heroin Street-life in Detroit." *Criminology* 24:645–66.

Miethe, T., M. Stafford, and J. Long. 1987. "Social Differentiation in Criminal Victimization: A Test of the Routine Activities/Lifestyle Theories." *American Sociological Review* 52:184–94.

Miller, G. 1989. *Down These Mean Streets: Violence By and Against America's Children.* Washington, DC: U.S. House of Representatives, Select Committee on Children, Youth, and Families.

Miller, W. B. 1958. "Lower Class Culture as a Generating Milieu of Gang Delinquency." *Journal of Social Issues* 14:5–19.

Miller, W., H. Geertz, and H. Cutter. 1961. "Aggression in a Boys' Street Corner Group." *Psychiatry* 24:283–98.

Moore, J. W. 1991. *Going Down to the Barrio: Homeboys and Homegirls in Change.* Philadelphia: Temple University Press.

Morash, M. 1983. "Gangs, Groups, and Delinquency." *British Journal of Criminology* 23:309–35.

Moynihan, D. 1993. "Guns Don't Kill People. Bullets Do." *New York Times,* 12 December.

National Center for Juvenile Justice. 1992. "Youth Murder Arrests Up Nearly 50 Percent, 1988–1990." Press release, 26 February, pp. 681–84.

National Institute of Education. 1978. *Violent Schools—Safe Schools: The Safe School Study Report to the Congress,* Vol. 1. Washington, DC: US Government Printing Office.

National School Boards Association. 1993. *Violence in the Schools.* Alexandria, VA: National School Boards Association.

National School Safety Center. 1989. *Safe Schools Overview.* Malibu, CA: National School Safety Center, Pepperdine University.

New Orleans Times-Picayune. 1991. "Bill Passed to Widen Schools' Powers to Search For Guns." 27 June.

New Orleans Times-Picayune. 1992. "Gangs In, Spies Out as FBI's Priority." 10 January.

New Orleans Times-Picayune. 1993. "Kids and Guns." 27 July.

New York Times. 1994. "Young People Are Victimized Most," 18 July.

Newsweek. 1992. "It's Not Just New York . . . " (March 9):25–29.

Nurco, D., T. Hanlon, T. Kinlock, and K. Duszynski. 1988. "Differential Criminal patterns of Narcotic Addiction Over an Addiction Career." *Criminology* 26:407–23.

O'Brien, R. 1985. *Crime and Victimization Data.* Beverly Hills, CA: Sage.

Osofsky, J., S. Wewers, D. Hann, and A. Fick. 1993. "Chronic Community Violence: What Is Happening to Our Children?" *Psychiatry* 56:36–45.

Padilla, F. 1992. *The Gang as an American Enterprise.* New Brunswick, NJ: Rutgers.

Parker, R., W. Smith, D. Smith, and J. Toby. 1991. "Trends in Victimization in Schools and Elsewhere." *Journal of Quantitative Criminology* 7:3–17.

Pearson, F. and J. Toby. 1991. "Fear of School-Related Predatory Crime." *Sociology and Social Research* 75:117–25.

Polsby, D. 1994. "The False Promise: Gun Control and Crime." *Atlantic Monthly* 273:57–70.

Pooley, E. 1991. "Kids With Guns." *New York Magazine* (August 5):20–29.

Popkin, J. 1991. "Bombs Over America." *U.S. News and World Report* (July 29):18–20.

Rand, M. 1990. *Handgun Crime Victims*. Washington, DC: Bureau of Justice Statistics.

Reinhold, R. 1988. "In the Middle of L.A.'s Gang Warfare." *New York Times Magazine* (May 22):30–33.

Reiss, A. and J. Roth. 1993. *Understanding and Preventing Violence*. Washington, DC: National Academy Press.

Rich, J. 1981. "School Violence: Four Theories Explain Why It Happens." *NASSP Bulletin* (November):64–71.

Rich, J. 1982. *Discipline and Authority in School and Family*. Lexington, MA: Heath.

Rose, H. M. and P. D. McClain. 1990. *Race, Place, and Risk: Black Homicide in Urban America*. Albany, NY: SUNY Press.

Sadowski, L., R. Cairns, and J. Earp. 1989. "Firearm Ownership among Nonurban Adolescents." *American Journal of Diseases of Children* 143:1410–13.

Sampson, R. 1985. "Sex Differences in Self-Reported Delinquency and Official Records: A Multiple-Group Structural Modeling Approach." *Journal of Quantitative Criminology* 1:345–68.

Scholastic Update. 1991. "Young and Deadly: The Rise in Teen Violence" (April 5):2–23.

Schubiner, H., R. Scott, and A. Tzelepis. 1993. "Exposure to Violence among Inner-City Youth." *American Journal of Diseases of Children* 146:214–19.

Scott, K. 1993. *Monster: The Autobiography of an L.A. Gang Member*. New York: Penguin.

Sheley, J. and V. E. Brewer. 1995. "Possession and Carrying of Firearms Among Suburban Youth." *Public Health Reports* 110:18–26.

Sheley, J., Z. McGee, and J. Wright. 1992. "Gun-Related Violence in and around Inner-City Schools." *American Journal of Diseases of Children* 146:677–82.

Short, J. F. and F. L. Strodtbeck. 1965. *Group Process and Gang Delinquency*. Chicago: University of Chicago Press.

Skogan, W. 1978. "Weapon Use in Robbery." In *Violent Crime: Historical and Contemporary Issues,* edited by J. Inciardi and A. Pottieger. Beverly Hills, CA: Sage.

Skogan, W. 1990. *Disorder and Decline.* New York: Free Press.

Skolnick, J., R. Bluthenthal, and T. Correl. 1993. "Gang Organization and Migration." Pp. 193–217 in *Gangs,* edited by Scott Cummings and Daniel J. Monti. Albany, NY: SUNY Press.

Smith, D. M. and J. F. Sheley (1995). "Possession and Carrying of Firearms among a Sample of Inner-City High School Females." *Journal of Crime and Justice.*

Snyder, H. N. 1992. "Arrests of Youth 1990." *Juvenile Justice Bulletin* (January). Office of Juvenile Justice and Delinquency Prevention, Washington, DC.

Spergel, I. 1964. *Slumtown, Racketville, Haulburg.* Chicago: University of Chicago Press.

Spergel, I. 1983. *Violent Gangs in Chicago: Segmentation and Integration.* Chicago: University of Chicago, School of Social Service Administration.

Spergel, I. 1989. *Youth Gangs: A Review of the Literature.* Chicago: University of Chicago, School of Social Service Administration.

Spergel, I. 1990. "Youth Gangs: Continuity and Change." Pp. 171–275 in *Crime and Justice,* Vol. 12, edited by M. Tonry and N. Morris. Chicago: University of Chicago Press.

Spergel, I., R. Chance, and G. Curry. 1990. "National Youth Gang Suppression and Intervention Program." *Juvenile Justice Bulletin.* Office of Juvenile Justice and Delinquency Prevention, Washington, DC.

Spergel, I., G. Curry, R. Ross, and R. Chance (eds.). 1989. *Survey: National Youth Gang Suppression and Intervention Project.* Chicago: University of Chicago, School of Social Service Administration.

Steffensmeier, D. and E. Allan. 1995. "Criminal Behavior: Gender and Age." Pp. 83–113 in *Criminology: A Contemporary Handbook,* edited by J. Sheley. Belmont, CA: Wadsworth.

Stephens, R. D. 1989. "Gangs, Guns, and Drugs." *School Safety* (Fall): 16–17.

Stumphauzer, J. S., E. V. Veloz, and T. W. Aiken. 1981. "Violence by Street Gangs: East Side Story?" In *Violent Behavior: Street Learning Approaches to Prediction, Management, and Treatment,* edited by R. B. Stuart. New York: Brunner-Mazel.

Taylor, C. 1990. "Gang Imperialism." Pp. 103–15 in *Gangs in America,* edited by C. Ronald Huff. Newbury Park, CA: Sage.

Thistle, F. 1974. "Maybe It's Time We Discussed Violence in America's Schools." *PTA Magazine* 1(October):15–17.

Thornberry, T., M. Krohn, A. Lizotte, and D. Wierschem. 1993. "The

Role of Juvenile Gangs in Facilitating Delinquent Behavior." *Journal of Research in Crime and Delinquency* 30:355–87.

Thrasher, F. 1936. *The Gang*, 2nd ed. Chicago: University of Chicago Press.

Time. 1989. "Shootouts in the Schools" (November 20):116.

Time. 1993. "A Boy and His Gun" (August 2):21–27.

Tracy, P. 1987. *Subcultural Delinquency: A Comparison of the Incidence and Severity of Gang and Nongang Member Offenses*. Boston: Northeastern University, College of Criminal Justice.

Treaster, J. and M. Taylor. 1992. "Teen-Age Gunslinging Is on Rise, in Search of Protection and Profit." *New York Times*, 17 February.

U.S. Department of Education. 1984. *Disorder in Our Public Schools*. Washington, DC: Department of Education.

U.S. Department of Health and Human Services. 1991. *Morbidity and Mortality Weekly Report: Weapon-Carrying among High School—United States, 1990*. Washington, DC: Department of Health and Human Services, Public Health Service.

U.S. Department of Justice. 1991. "More than 400,000 Students Were Violent Crime Victims During Six-Month Period in 1988 and 1989." *Department of Justice Press Release*, September 29.

U.S. Department of Justice. 1992. *Criminal Victimization in the United States, 1991*. Washington, DC: U.S. Department of Justice.

U.S. Department of Justice. 1988. *Profile of State Prison Inmates, 1986*. Washington, DC: Department of Justice, Bureau of Justice Statistics.

U.S. Public Health Service. 1992. *Violent and Abusive Youth*. Washington, DC: U.S. Department of Health and Human Services, Public Health Service.

U.S. News and World Report. 1990. "Your Jacket or Your Life" (February 6):14.

U.S. News and World Report. 1993. "Violence in Schools" November 8: 31–36.

U.S. Senate, Committee on the Judiciary, Majority Staff Report. 1991. *1991 Murder Toll: Initial Projections*. Washington, DC: United States Senate, Committee on the Judiciary.

Vigil, J. 1990. "Cholos and Gangs: Culture Change and Street Youth in Los Angeles." Pp. 116–28 in *Gangs in America*, edited by R. Huff. Newbury Park, CA: Sage.

Visher, C. 1991. "Career Offenders and Selective Incapacitation." Pp. 459–77 in *Criminology: A Contemporary Handbook*, edited by J. Sheley. Belmont, CA: Wadsworth.

Wallace, M. and J. Rothschild. 1988. "Plant Closings, Capital Flight, and Worker Dislocation: The Long Shadow of Deindustrialization." Pp.

1–35 in *Research in Politics and Society,* Vol. 3, edited by M. Wallace and J. Rothschild. Greenwich, CT: JAI.

Washington Post. 1992. "A D.C. Neighborhood under Siege," 19 November.

Webster, D., P. Gainer, and H. Champion. 1993. "Weapon Carrying among Inner-City Junior High School Students: Defensive Behavior vs. Aggressive Behavior." *American Journal of Public Health* 83: 1604–8.

Whitaker, C. and L. Bastion. 1991. *Teenage Victims: A National Crime Survey Report.* Washington, DC: Department of Justice.

White, H., V. Johnson, and C. Garrison. 1985. "The Drugs-Crime Nexus among Adolescents and Their Peers." *Deviant Behavior* 6:183–204.

White, H., R. Pandina, and R. LaGrange. 1987. "Longitudinal Predictors of Serious Substance Use and Delinquency." *Criminology* 25:715–40.

Williams, T. and W. Kornblum. 1985. *Growing Up Poor.* Lexington, MA: Lexington Books.

Wilson, W. J. 1987. *The Truly Disadvantaged: The Inner City, the Underclass, and Public Policy.* Chicago: University of Chicago Press.

Wish, E. and B. Johnson. 1986. "The Impact of Substance Abuse on Criminal Careers." Pp. 52–88 in *Criminal Careers and "Career Criminals,"* Vol. 2, edited by Blumstein, A., J. Cohen, J. Roth, and C. Visher. Washington, DC: National Academy Press.

Witkin, G. 1991. "Kids Who Kill." *U.S. News and World Report* (April 8):26–32.

Wolff, C. 1990. "Guns Offer New York Teen-Agers A Commonplace, Deadly Allure." *New York Times,* 5 November.

Wolfgang, M., T. Thornberry, and R. Figlio. 1987. *From Boy to Man, from Delinquency to Crime.* Chicago: University of Chicago Press.

Wright, J. and J. Devine. 1994. *Drugs as a Social Problem.* New York: Harper Collins.

Wright, J. and P. Rossi. 1986. *Armed and Considered Dangerous.* Hawthorne, NY: Aldine.

Wright, J., P. Rossi, and K. Daly. 1983. *Under the Gun.* Hawthorne, NY: Aldine.

AUTHOR INDEX

SUBJECT INDEX

Acquisition (of guns) by juveniles, 46–50
Addiction (*see* Drugs)
Alcohol use, 21–22, 37 (*see also* Drugs)
Ammunition, 162
Arrest records (of sample), 30
Assault weapons, 9, 10, 39
  and drug dealing, 75
Attitudes towards violence, 29–30, 37, 74

Brady Law, 54, 151

Carrying guns, 42–43, 62–63, 65–67
  among gang members, 102
  likely situations for, 65
  reasons for, 67
Correctional facilities, 16
Cost of guns, 49
Crime
  and drug sales, 76
  and drug use, 76
  and guns, 11, 57–63, 93
  armed robbery, 58–60
Crime Bill (1994), 149
Criminality
  burglary, 29
  robbery, 29
  self-reported, 24
  sample profiles, 27–35, 73
Criminals
  gun acquisition among adult, 9

Dangerous environment, 27
  and gangs, 110–113

and victimization, 128–129, 145
description of sample's, 27–30
effects on gun behavior,
in suburbs, 137
Dropouts and weapons, 7
Drugs
  dealers, users, and the firearms supply, 46
  use within sample, 18, 19, 25, 31–32, 78
  student sample, 25, 78
  inmate sample, 25, 78
  sales, 8, 11, 21, 32, 34, 36, 76–77, 78
  and gangs (*see* Gangs)
  and gun activity, 83–86
  and guns, 8, 9, 10, 22, 75–93, 125–126, 154–156
  and predatory crime, 86–89
  and violence, 22, 76–77
Drug use score, 32, 78

Enforcement of gun laws, 150

Families (of respondents)
  characteristics, 35–36
  gun ownership, 27, 29
  as gun suppliers, 46
  incarceration among, 28
Fear of violence (*see* Violence)
Females and guns, 35, 119–126
  drugs and guns, 125–126
  exposure to firearms, 120–122
  firearm acquisition, 124–125
  gangs and guns, 126